AZ-900 Exam Prep

500 Practice Questions

1st Edition

www.versatileread.com

Document Control

Proposal Name	:	AZ-900 Exam Prep: 500 Practice Questions
Document Edition	:	1st
Document Release Date	:	7th June 2024
Reference	:	AZ-900
VR Product Code	:	20241702AZ900

Feedback:

If you have any comments regarding the quality of this book or otherwise alter it to better suit your needs, you can contact us through email at info@versatileread.com

Please make sure to include the book's title and ISBN in your message.

About the Contributors:

Nouman Ahmed Khan

AWS/Azure/GCP-Architect, CCDE, CCIEx5 (R&S, SP, Security, DC, Wireless), CISSP, CISA, CISM, CRISC, ISO27K-LA is a Solution Architect working with a global telecommunication provider. He works with enterprises, mega-projects, and service providers to help them select the best-fit technology solutions. He also works as a consultant to understand customer business processes and helps select an appropriate technology strategy to support business goals. He has more than eighteen years of experience working with global clients. One of his notable experiences was his tenure with a large managed security services provider, where he was responsible for managing the complete MSSP product portfolio. With his extensive knowledge and expertise in various areas of technology, including cloud computing, network infrastructure, security, and risk management, Nouman has become a trusted advisor for his clients.

Abubakar Saeed

Abubakar Saeed is a trailblazer in the realm of technology and innovation. With a rich professional journey spanning over twenty-nine years, Abubakar has seamlessly blended his expertise in engineering with his passion for transformative leadership. Starting humbly at the grassroots level, he has significantly contributed to pioneering the Internet in Pakistan and beyond. Abubakar's multifaceted experience encompasses managing, consulting, designing, and implementing projects, showcasing his versatility as a leader.

His exceptional skills shine in leading businesses, where he champions innovation and transformation. Abubakar stands as a testament to the power of visionary leadership, heading operations, solutions design, and integration. His emphasis on adhering to project timelines and exceeding customer expectations has set him apart as a great leader. With an unwavering commitment to adopting technology for operational simplicity and enhanced efficiency, Abubakar Saeed continues to inspire and drive change in the industry.

Dr. Fahad Abdali

Dr. Fahad Abdali is an esteemed leader with an outstanding twenty-year track record in managing diverse businesses. With a stellar educational background, including a bachelor's degree from the prestigious NED University of Engineers & Technology and a Ph.D. from the University of Karachi, Dr. Abdali epitomizes academic excellence and continuous professional growth.

Dr. Abdali's leadership journey is marked by his unwavering commitment to innovation and his astute understanding of industry dynamics. His ability to navigate intricate challenges has driven growth and nurtured organizational triumph. Driven by a passion for excellence, he stands as a beacon of inspiration within the business realm. With his remarkable leadership skills, Dr. Fahad Abdali continues to steer businesses toward unprecedented success, making him a true embodiment of a great leader.

Muniza Kamran

Muniza Kamran is a technical content developer in a professional field. She crafts clear and informative content that simplifies complex technical concepts for diverse audiences, with a passion for technology. Her expertise lies in Microsoft, cybersecurity, cloud security and emerging technologies, making her a valuable asset in the tech industry. Her dedication to quality and accuracy ensures that her writing empowers readers with valuable insights and knowledge. She has done certification in SQL database, database design, cloud solution architecture, and NDG Linux unhatched from CISCO.

Table of Contents

About AZ-900 Certification 6

    Introduction 6

    What is AZ-900? 6

    Benefits of AZ-900 6

    Prerequisites for the AZ-900 Exam 7

    The intended audience for the AZ-900 Certification Course? 7

    The certification Exam 8

    Exam Preparation 8

        Before Exam 8

        Day of Exam 9

        After Exam... 9

    Exam Information... 10

    AZ-900 Exam Preparation Pointers... 10

    Prerequisites.. 11

    Recertification... 12

    Job Opportunities with AZ-900 Certifications 12

        IT Support Roles 12

        Cloud Administration Roles (Entry-Level) 12

        Other Potential Opportunities 13

    Demand for AZ-900 Certification in 2024 13

Practice Questions.. 14

Answers 122

About Our Products 224

About AZ-900 Certification

Introduction

This chapter introduces the AZ-900 certification, which plays a crucial role in understanding the fundamentals of Microsoft Azure cloud computing. It underlines the advantages of obtaining AZ-900 certification, provides an overview of the certification process, and highlights the significance of adhering to ethical principles. Moreover, it discusses the rising demand for professionals with AZ-900 certification in the continually evolving field of cloud computing, paving the way for in-depth exploration of exam readiness strategies and career opportunities.

What is AZ-900?

AZ-900 is the Microsoft Azure Fundamentals certification exam. It validates a candidate's foundational knowledge of cloud services and how those services are provided with Microsoft Azure. The exam covers basic concepts of cloud computing, core Azure services, security, privacy, compliance, and Azure pricing and support. Passing the AZ-900 exam demonstrates an understanding of cloud concepts and foundational Azure services, making it a valuable credential for individuals beginning their journey in cloud computing or seeking to validate their Azure knowledge.

Benefits of AZ-900

The AZ-900 Azure Fundamentals certification offers numerous advantages to individuals entering the realm of cloud computing. Firstly, it establishes a strong foundational knowledge of cloud computing concepts and core Azure services. This serves as a solid groundwork for further specialization within the Azure ecosystem. Secondly, AZ-900 certification enhances career prospects by bolstering credibility with potential employers, potentially unlocking new opportunities in Azure-related roles. Thirdly, achieving AZ-900 demonstrates a commitment to continuous learning and professional growth, garnering recognition from peers and industry stakeholders. Additionally, passing the exam validates proficiency in Azure services, instilling confidence in one's ability to work effectively in cloud environments.

Moreover, AZ-900 serves as a stepping stone to more advanced Azure certifications, paving the way for career advancement. Furthermore, preparing for AZ-900 fosters problem-solving skills and critical thinking, which are invaluable assets in cloud computing roles. Lastly, in a competitive job market, AZ-900 certification sets candidates apart, providing a competitive edge and increasing their likelihood of securing interviews and job opportunities in the dynamic field of cloud computing.

Prerequisites for the AZ-900 Exam

Prerequisites for excelling in the AZ-900 exam do not demand an extensive background. However, a strong grasp of foundational cloud service concepts, particularly those related to Azure, is crucial. Familiarizing yourself with Azure basics will significantly enhance your chances of success.

The intended audience for the AZ-900 Certification Course?

The intended audience for the AZ-900 Certification Course includes IT professionals new to Azure, aiming to acquire practical knowledge about Azure services and their direct application. Notably, scripting knowledge is not a prerequisite; the focus is on using the Azure portal and command line interface for resource creation. Additionally, students or beginners exploring Azure job opportunities can gain the confidence needed to pursue further role-based Azure programs, such as becoming an Azure Administrator.

The certification Exam

The AZ-900 (Microsoft Azure Fundamentals) certification exam evaluates candidates' understanding and proficiency in fundamental concepts of cloud computing with Microsoft Azure. This comprehensive assessment aims to measure candidates' grasp of key principles, terminology, and practices related to Azure cloud services.

- **Cloud Concepts and Principles**: This domain assesses candidates' comprehension of cloud computing concepts, including the benefits of cloud services, deployment models, and service models offered by Microsoft Azure.
- **Core Azure Services**: Candidates are evaluated on their knowledge of essential Azure services, such as computing, storage, networking, and databases, and their functionalities within the Azure ecosystem.
- **Azure Pricing and Support**: This domain focuses on candidates' understanding of Azure pricing models, subscription options, and support plans available to Azure customers.
- **Azure Security, Privacy, Compliance, and Trust**: Candidates must demonstrate their knowledge of Azure security principles, privacy controls, compliance standards, and trust mechanisms implemented by Microsoft to safeguard Azure services and data.
- **Azure Governance and Compliance**: This domain assesses candidates' comprehension of Azure governance methodologies, resource management techniques, and compliance considerations for managing Azure resources effectively.
- **Azure Service Level Agreements (SLAs) and Lifecycles**: Candidates are evaluated on their understanding of Azure SLAs, service lifecycles, and maintenance practices to ensure the high availability and reliability of Azure services.

Exam Preparation

Before Exam

To prepare for the AZ-900 exam, it is essential to start by thoroughly reviewing the exam content outline provided by Microsoft. This outline delineates the domains and topics that will be covered in the exam, giving you a clear roadmap of what to focus on. Once you have familiarized yourself with the content, it is time to dive into study materials. Utilize a variety of resources such as textbooks, official Microsoft documentation, online courses, and practice exams to reinforce your understanding of Microsoft Azure fundamentals.

Day of Exam

On exam day, it is crucial to arrive early at the exam center to allow for check-in procedures and to settle in before the exam begins. Be sure to bring along all required documents, including valid identification and any other materials specified by the exam center. Once the exam starts, maintain a calm and focused mindset. Take deep breaths to help manage any nerves, and read each question carefully to fully understand what is being asked. Avoid feeling overwhelmed by difficult questions by staying focused and maintaining confidence in your abilities.

Managing your time effectively is essential during the exam. Pace yourself to ensure you have enough time to answer all questions thoroughly. If you encounter particularly challenging questions, consider flagging them for review and returning to them later if time permits. By following these tips, you will be better equipped to navigate the exam confidently and achieve success.

After Exam

After completing the exam, it is important to take time to reflect on your performance. Identify areas where you excelled and areas where there is room for improvement. If you have access to your exam results, review any questions you missed to understand why you answered incorrectly and learn from your mistakes. This reflection process helps solidify your understanding of the material and prepares you for future exams or real-world scenarios.

Exam Information

Prior Certification Not Required		**Exam Validity** Lifetime	
Exam Fee $99 USD		**Exam Duration** 90 Minutes	
No. of Questions 40-60 Questions		**Passing Marks** 700	A+

Recommended Experience
Foundational knowledge of Cloud Services and Azure Services

Exam Format
Multiple Choice, Drag & drop, Case studies, Multiple response

AZ-900 Exam Preparation Pointers

Preparing for the Azure AZ-900 certification exam requires a structured approach to ensure readiness and confidence on exam day. Here are some tips to guide your AZ-900 exam preparation:

1. **Understand the Exam Content**: Familiarize yourself with the domains and topics outlined in the AZ-900 exam content provided by Microsoft. This will give you a clear understanding of what to expect on the exam and which areas to focus your study efforts on.
2. **Utilize Study Materials**: Make use of a variety of AZ-900 study materials, including textbooks, official Microsoft documentation, online courses, and practice exams. These resources will help reinforce your understanding of Azure fundamentals and provide insights into exam format and question types.
3. **Take Practice Exams**: Completing AZ-900 practice exams is essential for assessing your knowledge and identifying areas that

require further study. Practice exams simulate the exam environment and help you gauge your readiness while familiarizing yourself with the types of questions you may encounter.

4. **Create a Study Schedule**: Develop a study schedule that allocates time for reviewing each domain covered in the AZ-900 exam content. Set realistic study goals and deadlines to keep yourself accountable and ensure thorough coverage of all exam topics.

5. **Join Study Groups:** Consider joining AZ-900 study groups or online forums where you can engage with other exam candidates, share resources, and discuss challenging topics. Collaborating with peers can provide additional insights and support throughout your exam preparation journey.

6. **Stay Updated:** Keep abreast of developments in Azure fundamentals by staying updated with industry trends, best practices, and emerging technologies. Attend relevant training sessions, workshops, and conferences to expand your knowledge and skills in this evolving field.

7. **Practice Time Management:** During the exam, manage your time effectively by pacing yourself and allocating sufficient time to answer each question. Flag difficult questions for review and prioritize your efforts based on question weight and difficulty.

Prerequisites

There is no prior certification required for this course. However, Microsoft recommends some general skills and knowledge that may be beneficial before taking the AZ-900 course:

Familiarity with basic IT concepts: A general understanding of basic IT concepts, such as networking, storage, and computing, can be helpful.

Basic understanding of cloud computing: While not mandatory, having a basic awareness of cloud computing concepts will make it easier to grasp the content covered in the course.

Experience using internet browsers: The course materials and labs may involve using web-based interfaces, so familiarity with internet browsers is beneficial.

Recertification

The specific recertification requirements can vary depending on the certification track and the policies set by Microsoft. Here are some general points regarding recertification:

Certification Validity Period: Many Microsoft certifications, including the Azure certifications, have a validity period (usually two years). After this period, the certification may expire.

Recertification Exams: To maintain certification, individuals may need to pass a recertification exam or take a specific set of exams. Microsoft may update the certification exams to reflect changes in technology and services.

Job Opportunities with AZ-900 Certifications

The AZ-900 Microsoft Azure Fundamentals certification, while foundational, can open doors to various entry-level and foundational roles in the cloud computing field, particularly those focused on Microsoft Azure. Here is a breakdown of some potential opportunities:

IT Support Roles

- **Cloud Support Specialist:** Assisting users with basic Azure cloud services and troubleshooting issues.
- **Technical Support Specialist:** Providing technical support for cloud-based applications or infrastructure.
- **IT Support Technician:** Offering general IT support with a potential focus on cloud-related inquiries.

Cloud Administration Roles (Entry-Level)

- **Junior Cloud Administrator:** Performing basic cloud administration tasks under supervision, such as user provisioning and resource management.
- **Cloud Operations Specialist:** Assisting with cloud deployments, monitoring, and basic troubleshooting.

Other Potential Opportunities

- **Cloud Sales Specialist:** Leveraging your understanding of Azure fundamentals to explain cloud benefits to potential customers.
- **Business Analyst:** Utilizing cloud knowledge to analyze business needs and identify potential cloud solutions.
- **Project Coordinator:** Coordinating cloud-related projects, ensuring tasks align with Azure functionalities.

Demand for AZ-900 Certification in 2024

The demand for the AZ-900 Microsoft Azure Fundamentals certification is expected to remain strong in 2024 for several reasons:

- **Cloud Adoption Growth:** Cloud computing continues to experience significant adoption across businesses of all sizes. As companies migrate to the cloud, the need for professionals with a foundational understanding of Azure services will persist.
- **Entry Point to Azure Expertise:** AZ-900 serves as the launching pad for any Azure certification path. Earning this credential demonstrates a basic grasp of cloud concepts and Azure functionalities, making it valuable for anyone interested in pursuing a cloud career.
- **Validation of Basic Skills:** Even for non-technical roles, having an AZ-900 certification showcases a basic understanding of cloud computing, potentially giving you an edge in today's job market.

Practice Questions

1. What is the primary function of cloud computing?
A. To provide physical hardware to companies
B. To rent resources like storage space or CPU cycles
C. To sell software licenses
D. To maintain user's personal computers

2. What is a virtual machine (VM)?
A. A physical server in a data center
B. An emulation of a computer system
C. A storage space for files
D. A type of cloud service

3. How is a virtual machine different from a physical computer?
A. It requires more maintenance
B. It cannot run software
C. It is hosted on a cloud provider's server
D. It has its physical hardware

4. What are containers in cloud computing?
A. A data storage solution
B. A type of virtual machine with a guest OS
C. Packages that include an application and its dependencies
D. Physical shipping containers used in data centers

5. What is serverless computing?
A. Renting servers from a cloud provider
B. Running application code without maintaining a server
C. A service for server maintenance

D. A computer without servers

6. Which computing model is ideal for automated tasks?
A. Virtual Machines
B. Containers
C. Serverless Computing
D. Physical servers

7. How are VMs and containers charged in the cloud?
A. By the amount of data that they store
B. While they are running, even if idle
C. Only when the applications on them are active
D. Based on the number of users accessing them

8. What is the main advantage of using a virtual machine within the cloud?
A. It eliminates the need for an operating system
B. It requires less time to set up compared to a physical computer
C. It offers unlimited physical storage
D. It does not share resources with other VMs

9. How does serverless computing charge for processing time?
A. By the hour
B. By the minute
C. By the amount of data processed
D. Only for the time used by each function as it executes

10. What is not a popular computing choice in cloud computing?
A. Virtual Machines
B. Containers
C. Serverless computing

D. Distributed databases

11. What cloud computing pricing model is described in the provided text?
A. Fixed pricing model
B. Pay-as-you-go
C. Subscription-based
D. One-time payment

12. What is meant by 'scaling up' in the context of cloud computing?
A. Adding more servers
B. Increasing network bandwidth
C. Adding resources to an existing server
D. Reducing the number of servers

13. What is the benefit of cloud computing's elastic nature?
A. Fixed costs for resources
B. Automatic updates to software
C. Automatic adjustment of resources based on demand
D. Increased security measures

14. Why is cloud computing considered 'current' according to the text?
A. It provides a global presence
B. It supports high data traffic
C. It eliminates the burden of IT management tasks
D. It uses the latest hardware

15. How does cloud computing assure the reliability of data?
A. By providing unlimited data storage
B. By offering data backup and disaster recovery services

C. By using a fixed pricing model

D. By enabling vertical scaling

16. What feature of cloud computing enhances fault tolerance?

A. Automatic resource allocation

B. Pay-as-you-go pricing

C. Redundancy in cloud services architecture

D. Manual scaling

17. How does cloud computing provide a global presence for services?

A. Through a single centralized data center

B. By using the latest software

C. By having data centers in various regions across the globe

D. By offering a fixed bandwidth globally

18. What type of scaling involves adding more servers that function together?

A. Vertical scaling

B. Diagonal scaling

C. Horizontal scaling

D. Static scaling

19. Why can cloud providers offer better security than many organizations?

A. Due to the nature of vertical scaling

B. Because of the pay-as-you-go model

C. Owing to expert technical skills and comprehensive security measures

D. Through its reliance on manual updates

20. What can be done automatically in cloud computing based on specific triggers such as CPU utilization?

A. Data backup

B. Resource scaling
C. Global data center replication
D. Software patching

21. What does CapEx stand for in financial terms?
A. Capital Expenditure
B. Capital Expansion
C. Capital Experience
D. Capital Execution

22. How does OpEx differ from CapEx in terms of payment?
A. OpEx requires a significant upfront cost
B. OpEx is considered an investment in physical assets
C. OpEx allows for immediate deduction from the tax bill
D. OpEx expenses are depreciated over time

23. Which of the following is a benefit of CapEx?
A. Costs fluctuate along with demand
B. There's no upfront cost
C. Expenses are planned at the start of a project
D. Costs are managed dynamically

24. When would OpEx be more appealing compared to CapEx?
A. When the demand is consistent and known
B. When there's a need for significant upfront investment in infrastructure
C. When the demand fluctuates or is unknown
D. When costs need to be fixed for the duration of a project

25. What does OpEx typically include in the context of cloud computing?
A. Purchasing servers and storage hardware

B. Leasing cloud-based server and software
C. Building a data center infrastructure
D. Hiring technical personnel as permanent staff

26. What type of cost is associated with leasing a data center infrastructure?
A. OpEx
B. CapEx
C. Both OpEx and CapEx
D. Neither OpEx nor CapEx

27. Which expenditure type is characterized by having no upfront cost?
A. CapEx
B. OpEx
C. Both OpEx and CapEx
D. Neither OpEx nor CapEx

28. What is one of the economies of scale consider as   in the context of cloud computing?
A. Higher costs per unit with increased scale
B. Lower cost per unit when operating at a larger scale
C. Fixed costs regardless of scale
D. Upfront costs increase with scale

29. In terms of tax deductions, how does CapEx differ from OpEx?
A. CapEx allows for immediate deduction, whereas OpEx deductions are spread over time
B. CapEx is not deductible, while OpEx is deductible in the same year
C. CapEx deductions are spread over time, whereas OpEx allows for immediate deduction
D. There is no difference in tax deductions between CapEx and OpEx

30. Why might a business choose CapEx over OpEx for a project?
A. To avoid any upfront costs
B. To ensure expenses fluctuate with demand
C. To have unpredictable costs throughout the project
D. To predict expenses before a project starts

31. What is one of the main advantages of using a public cloud deployment model?
A. You own the hardware and services
B. High scalability and agility
C. You are responsible for maintenance or updates of the hardware
D. You can easily manage legacy applications

32. What is the disadvantage of using a public cloud when it comes to security?
A. High scalability/agility
B. Pay-as-you-go pricing
C. The public cloud might not meet security requirements
D. Minimal technical knowledge required for setup

33. When might a private cloud deployment be necessary?
A. When there is no need for initial CapEx costs
B. When the organization has minimal technical knowledge
C. When you need to control and meet strict security, compliance, or legal requirements
D. When you want to rely on a third party for managing the infrastructure

34. What is the disadvantage of the private cloud in terms of costs?
A. High scalability/agility
B. Pay-as-you-go pricing
C. Some initial CapEx costs for startup and maintenance

D. Economies at scale

35. What can a hybrid cloud deployment offer in terms of hardware or operating systems?
A. It requires no CapEx costs
B. It cannot combine public and private cloud resources
C. It can keep systems running that use out-of-date hardware or operating systems
D. It simplifies the setup and management processes

36. What is one of the benefits of a hybrid cloud in terms of cost?
A. Unlimited CapEx costs
B. Economies of scale from public cloud providers
C. High initial investment in hardware
D. No need for IT skills and expertise

37. Which cloud deployment model allows for maximum control over the environment?
A. Public cloud
B. Hybrid cloud
C. Private cloud
D. All of the above

38. What is the disadvantage of hybrid clouds in terms of complexity?
A. They provide minimal technical knowledge requirements
B. They have lower agility than public clouds
C. They can be more complicated to set up and manage
D. They do not require IT skills and expertise

39. How does a private cloud deployment model compare to a public cloud in terms of agility?

A. Private cloud offers higher agility than public cloud

B. Private cloud agility is limited by the necessity to purchase and set up new hardware

C. Private and public clouds offer the same level of agility

D. Public cloud requires more time to scale than private cloud

40. Why might an organization choose a hybrid cloud to meet business requirements?

A. To avoid any CapEx costs

B. To eliminate the need for IT expertise

C. To use their equipment for specific security or legacy scenarios

D. To ensure they have no control over security

41. What was Infrastructure as a Service (IaaS) primarily designed to provide?

A. A development platform for software applications

B. Centralized software management for end customers

C. Complete control over the hardware that runs your application

D. A managed platform for running software applications

42. Which of the following is a characteristic of a Platform as a Service (PaaS)?

A. Users manage the operating systems

B. Users rent hardware on a subscription basis

C. Users focus on application development without managing the underlying infrastructure

D. Users are responsible for managing everything, including the application software

43. What is a typical payment model for Software as a Service (SaaS)?

A. One-time payment for permanent access

B. Pay-per-use for each service used

C. Subscription-based, typically monthly or annually

D. High upfront costs for long-term use

44. Who is responsible for operating system management in a PaaS offering?

A. The user

B. The cloud provider

C. A third-party service

D. It is shared between the user and the cloud provider

45. In an IaaS model, what are the user's management responsibilities?

A. Only the applications and data they run and store

B. The hardware and networking components

C. The operating systems, data, and applications

D. Managing everything, including the application software

46. Which cloud service model requires the least amount of management from the user?

A. IaaS

B. PaaS

C. SaaS

D. All require the same amount of management.

47. What is the main advantage of using PaaS over IaaS?

A. Lower upfront costs

B. Full control over hardware

C. Less user management required

D. Responsibility for managing the operating systems

48. What do users pay for when they opt for IaaS?

A. A permanent software license

B. Ownership of the hardware
C. What they consume in terms of infrastructure
D. A fixed monthly fee for unlimited infrastructure usage

49. Which of the following best describes the responsibility of a SaaS user?
A. Managing the provision and maintenance of the application software
B. Developing their applications within the SaaS environment
C. Using the application software without maintenance or management responsibilities
D. Managing their data and applications while the cloud provider manages the infrastructure

50. How are PaaS and IaaS related in terms of service layers?
A. PaaS is a subset of IaaS with additional services
B. PaaS and IaaS operate independently with no overlap
C. PaaS replaces the need for IaaS completely
D. IaaS provides the infrastructure that PaaS builds upon

51. What service does Azure offer for running containerized services with a cluster of VMs?
A. Azure Virtual Machines
B. Azure Functions
C. Azure Kubernetes Service
D. Azure Container Instances

52. Which Azure service is used for load balancing inbound and outbound connections to applications or service endpoints?
A. Azure Virtual Network
B. Azure Load Balancer
C. Azure Traffic Manager

D. Azure VPN Gateway

53. What type of storage does Azure Blob Storage provide?
A. NoSQL data storage
B. File shares are accessible like a file server
C. Storage for very large objects like video files
D. A data store for queuing messages between applications

54. Which Azure service offers a fully managed relational database with auto-scale and advanced security features?
A. Azure SQL Database
B. Azure Cosmos DB
C. Azure Database for PostgreSQL
D. Azure Table storage

55. Azure IoT Hub serves what primary purpose in IoT solutions?
A. It provides a fully managed global IoT SaaS solution
B. It is a messaging hub for secure communications between IoT devices
C. It pushes data analysis on IoT devices
D. It is a managed service for IoT device caching

56. Which service in Azure is specialized for collaborative, drag-and-drop machine learning model building?
A. Azure Machine Learning Service
B. Azure Machine Learning Studio
C. Azure Cognitive Services
D. Azure Databricks

57. What is the role of Azure Content Delivery Network?
A. To connect VMs to VPN connections

B. To distribute network traffic across Azure regions

C. To deliver high-bandwidth content globally

D. To monitor and diagnose network issues

58. What is Azure ExpressRoute used for?

A. Balancing network traffic

B. Providing ultra-fast DNS responses

C. Connecting to Azure over high-bandwidth dedicated connections

D. Protecting against DDoS attacks

59. Azure SQL Data Warehouse is best suited for which scenario?

A. Hosting NoSQL databases

B. Running high-performance computing applications

C. Running analytics at a massive scale

D. Sending push notifications to any platform

60. Which Azure service aids in adding real-time web functionalities easily?

A. Azure SignalR Service

B. Azure App Service

C. Azure Notification Hubs

D. Azure API Management

61. What is Azure Cloud Shell?

A. A cloud storage service

B. A browser-based command-line experience for Azure

C. A desktop application for Azure management

D. A physical console for Azure servers

62. Which of the following experiences can be chosen within Azure Cloud Shell?

A. Bash

B. PowerShell

C. Both Bash and PowerShell

D. Visual Basic

63. What command is used to create a resource group in Azure using Azure CLI?

A. az group create

B. az vm create

C. az resource-group create

D. az create a group

64. What are the default configurations of a VM created with the following command:

az vm create \--name myVM \--resource-group Learn-ed49b49c-4d23-418b-89c2-7d6186579226 \--image Win2019Datacenter \--size Standard_DS2_v2 \--location eastus?

A. Windows Server 2019 image, 4 CPUs, and 16 GB of memory

B. Windows 10 image, 2 CPUs, and 7 GB of memory

C. Windows Server 2019 image, 2 CPUs, and 7 GB of memory

D. Linux image, 2 CPUs, and 7 GB of memory

65. How can you verify that a VM is running using Azure CLI?

A. By using the 'az vm check' command

B. By logging into the Azure portal

C. By using the 'az vm get-instance-view' command

D. By physically checking the Azure data center

66. Which Azure CLI command assigns a public IP address to a VM by default?
A. az network create
B. az vm create
C. az ip assign
D. az public-ip create

67. In Azure, what is a 'region'?
A. A specific operating system available for VMs
B. A named set of permissions for resource access
C. A set of Azure data centers in a named geographic location
D. A type of virtual machine size

68. What does the 'size' of a VM define in Azure?
A. The physical space it occupies in a data center
B. The processor speed, amount of memory, initial storage, and network bandwidth
C. The cost per hour of running the VM
D. The number of users that can access the VM

69. What is the purpose of resource groups in Azure?
A. To group user accounts into administrative units
B. To organize sets of resources that are deployed together as part of an application or service
C. To provide a collection of tools for developing Azure resources
D. To serve as a template for creating virtual machines

70. What is the primary function of Internet Information Services (IIS)?
A. To act as a database server

B. To serve web content like HTML, CSS, and JavaScript
C. To provide email services
D. To manage network traffic

71. How can you automate the deployment on Azure VMs?
A. Using the Microsoft Entra ID
B. With the Custom Script Extension
C. Using Azure Blob Storage only
D. Through manual configuration only

72. What is the command to set a Custom Script Extension in Azure VM?
A. az vm set-script
B. az vm extension add
C. az vm extension set
D. az vm script deploy

73. Which PowerShell command is used to install IIS on a Windows Server?
A. Install-WindowsFeature IIS-WebServerRole
B. enable-iis
C. dism /online /enable-feature /feature name: IIS-WebServerRole
D. setup-iis

74. What command should be run to allow inbound network access on port 80 for an Azure VM?
A. az vm open-port --port 80
B. az vm allow-http
C. az network firewall allows --port 80
D. az vm enable-port --http

75. What command can you use to list an Azure VM's public IP address?
A. az vm get-ip

B. az vm list-ip

C. az vm show --query [publicIps]

D. az network public-ip list

76. What would be the content of the home page after running the provided PowerShell script to configure IIS?

A. The default IIS welcome page

B. A custom message with the Azure logo

C. A basic home page with a welcome message and the VM's computer name

D. An error message indicating a misconfiguration

77. What is the purpose of the `--settings` parameter in the `az vm extension set` command?

A. To specify the VM's hardware settings

B. To define the network configuration

C. To indicate where to download scripts from

D. To provide the license information for the extension

78. What does the `--protected-settings` parameter in the `az vm extension set` command do?

A. It encrypts the entire PowerShell script

B. It specifies the execution policy and file to run on the VM

C. It sets up a password for the VM

D. It protects the VM from unauthorized access

79. What is the expected outcome after configuring IIS with the provided script and opening port 80?

A. The VM will restart automatically

B. The VM will start serving the custom home page over HTTP on port 80

C. FTP access will be granted to the VM

D. Remote desktop access will be enabled on the VM

80. What Azure CLI command is used to resize a virtual machine?
A. az vm change
B. az vm modify
C. az vm resize
D. az vm update

81. Which Azure service allows you to create and manage a set of virtual networks and gateways for secure communication between on-premises and Azure resources?
A. Azure ExpressRoute
B. Azure Virtual Network
C. Azure Traffic Manager
D. Azure VPN Gateway

82. Which of the following commands verifies the new size of the VM?
A. az vm list
B. az vm size
C. az vm show
D. az vm check

83. What is the output format specified in the 'az vm show' command?
A. JSON
B. YAML
C. TSV
D. XML

84. What Azure CLI command flag is used to specify the resource group of the VM?
A. --group

B. --resource-group

C. --group-resource

D. --vm-resource

85. Which component of the VM does the 'hardwareProfile' query specifically refer to?
A. CPU and memory allocation
B. Storage account type
C. Networking configuration
D. Operating system type

86 How do you specify the name of the VM when using the 'az vm resize' command?
A. --vm-name
B. --name
C. --vm
D. --name

87. What is the purpose of Azure Role-Based Access Control (RBAC)?

A. To encrypt data at rest
B. To manage user identities and access permissions
C. To automate the deployment of virtual machines
D. To backup and restore data

88. What is the purpose of the '--query "hardwareProfile"' part of the 'az vm show' command?
A. To list all hardware-related properties
B. To filter the output to only show the VM's storage profile
C. To filter the output to only show the VM's hardware profile
D. To query the VM's network profile

89. If you need to resize multiple VMs to the size Standard_DS3_v2, which of the following pieces of information must change in the command for each VM?
A. The resource group
B. The VM size
C. The VM name
D. The query

90. What is implied about getting involved with private or public previews?
A. It is compulsory for all Azure customers
B. It can help drive products in a useful direction for your organization
C. It is a paid service for advanced users only
D. It guarantees a feature will be included in the GA

91. What is an Azure region?
A. A single data center where Azure services are hosted
B. A specific service within Azure
C. A geographical area with multiple networked data centers
D. The physical location of Microsoft headquarters

92. What is the main benefit of Azure having more global regions than any other cloud provider?
A. Reduced costs for Microsoft
B. Increased competition among cloud providers
C. Flexibility in bringing applications closer to users
D. Simplified management of services

93. What is an Azure geography?
A. A single Azure region
B. A global network of Azure data centers

C. A discrete market defined by geopolitical boundaries
D. A collection of Azure services

94. Why are Azure geographies important?
A. They provide unlimited storage for data
B. They ensure data residency and compliance within geographical boundaries
C. They are used to categorize different Azure services
D. They reduce the cost of Azure services globally

95. What does data residency refer to in the context of Azure?
A. The number of data centers in a region
B. The location of Microsoft's corporate offices
C. The physical or geographic location of an organization's data
D. The residency status of Azure employees

96. How does Azure ensure fault tolerance at the geographical level?
A. By limiting the number of data centers in each region
B. Through high-capacity networking infrastructure connecting geographies
C. By offering free services
D. By using a single, centralized data center for backup

97. Which areas are Azure geographies broken up into?
A. North America, South America, and Central America
B. Americas, Europe, and Asia
C. Americas, Europe, Asia Pacific, Middle East, and Africa
D. Northern Hemisphere and Southern Hemisphere

98. What is the purpose of organizing Azure data centers into regions?
A. To limit the number of services Azure can offer
B. To reduce the overall cost of Azure services
C. To ensure workloads are balanced and provide scalability and redundancy
D. To restrict the use of Azure services to certain countries

99. Which of the following is a true statement about Azure regions?
A. Each Azure region is isolated from others and operates independently
B. Azure regions do not provide redundancy for deployed services
C. Users can directly access and choose specific data centers within a region
D. A region can contain multiple data centers networked together

100. What is the role of Availability Zones in Azure?
A. They are individual data centers with no special significance
B. They are unique services offered only in certain regions
C. They are single regions that contain multiple geographies
D. They are not mentioned in the provided context

101. What is the primary purpose of Availability Zones in Azure?
A. To provide a low-cost hosting solution
B. To ensure high availability and redundancy for hosted services
C. To offer automatic geo-redundant storage
D. To create single data center environments

102. What are Availability Zones comprised of?
A. Multiple regions within a geography
B. A single virtual machine
C. One or more data centers with independent power, cooling, and

networking
D. A group of virtual machines in the same data center

103. How are Availability Zones connected?
A. Through the public internet
B. With low-speed, shared networks
C. High-speed, private fiber-optic networks
D. Satellite communication

104. What is the SLA (Service Level Agreement) percentage for virtual machines in an Availability Set?
A. 99.99%
B. 99.95%
C. 99.9%
D. 100%

105. What SLA percentage do Availability Zones offer?
A. 99.95%
B. 99.9%
C. 99.99%
D. 100%

106. What is the minimum number of Availability Zones within a single Azure region?
A. One
B. Two
C. Three
D. Four

107. What is the difference between an Availability Zone and an Availability Set?
A. An Availability Zone is a low-cost hosting solution, whereas an Availability Set is not
B. An Availability Zone has a lower SLA than an Availability Set
C. An Availability Set is a group of virtual machines in the same data center, while an Availability Zone consists of virtual machines in different physical locations
D. Availability Sets are used for mission-critical applications, but Availability Zones are not

108. What is the purpose of Azure region pairs?
A. To provide redundancy within the same data center
B. To offer automatic scaling of resources
C. To reduce the likelihood of interruptions due to regional disasters
D. To connect Availability Zones within the same region

109. How far apart are region pairs typically located?
A. At least 100 miles
B. At least 200 miles
C. At least 300 miles
D. At least 400 miles

110. Which Azure service would you use to monitor and analyze the performance and health of your applications and services?

A. Azure DevOps
B. Azure Monitor
C. Azure Policy
D. Microsoft Defender for Cloud

111. What is the purpose of Service-Level Agreements (SLAs) with Azure?
A. To provide a legal framework for Azure customers
B. To define the performance standards for Azure products and services
C. To outline the pricing structure of Azure services
D. To describe new features in Azure services

112. What happens if an Azure service does not meet its SLA specifications?
A. The service is discontinued
B. Microsoft provides a full refund
C. Service credits are issued
D. Performance targets are adjusted

113. Which of the following is NOT a key characteristic of SLAs for Azure products and services?
A. Performance Targets
B. Uptime and Connectivity Guarantees
C. Service credits
D. Free upgrade to premium services

114. What are the typical performance target commitments specified in an SLA for Azure services?
A. 50-75 percent uptime
B. 75-90 percent uptime
C. 99-99.9 percent uptime
D. 99.9-99.999 percent uptime

115. What do SLAs for individual Azure products and services describe?
A. The customer's responsibilities
B. The physical location of Azure data centers
C. Microsoft's commitment to specific performance standards
D. The history of Azure service development

116. How are performance targets for some Azure services expressed?
A. As a fixed number of transactions
B. As uptime guarantees or connectivity rates
C. In terms of customer satisfaction scores
D. As a percentage of successful API calls

117. Is it possible to test the next version of the Azure portal?
A. Yes, but only after GA
B. No, it is not available for testing
C. Yes, it is available for public preview
D. Yes, it is available in private preview only

118. Are SLAs for Azure products and services standardized across all products?
A. Yes, they are the same for all services
B. No, they are specific to each Azure product and service
C. Yes, but only for related services
D. No, they are the same for all cloud providers

119. What type of Azure service metric might be included in an SLA?
A. Number of new features added each year
B. Customer service response times
C. Uptime or response times for services
D. Frequency of software updates

120. If an Azure service has a performance target of 99.9% uptime, how is this referred to in SLA terminology?
A. Two nines
B. Three nines

C. Four nines
D. Five nines

121. What is a Composite SLA?
A. A single SLA for the highest available service
B. The combined SLA when using multiple Azure services
C. A discounted SLA offering from Microsoft
D. A special SLA for enterprise-level customers

122. What is the approximate composite SLA when combining a service with a 99.95% SLA and another with a 99.99999% SLA?
A. 99.94%
B. 99.995%
C. 99.95%
D. 100%

123. What can happen if an Azure product or service does not meet its SLA?
A. Microsoft may provide technical support
B. Customers may receive a discount on their Azure bill
C. The service will be discontinued immediately
D. Customers will be charged extra for the downtime

124. How can application reliability be improved in relation to SLAs?
A. By avoiding the use of SLAs altogether
B. By ignoring service failures
C. By creating fallback paths in the application architecture
D. By using only a single Azure service

40

125. What is the purpose of an Application SLA?

A. To set minimum performance targets for Microsoft

B. To enforce penalties on Azure services

C. To establish performance targets suited to a specific Azure application

D. To guarantee 100% uptime for all services

126. How does resiliency relate to system failures?

A. It focuses on avoiding failures completely

B. It involves the system's ability to recover from failures

C. It is about predicting failures before they happen

D. It refers to the permanent fix of all system issues

127. What are two crucial components of resiliency?

A. High availability and low latency

B. Data migration and system upgrades

C. High availability and disaster recovery

D. System monitoring and regular backups

128. What is not guaranteed about preview features?

A. That they will be free of charge

B. That they will be advertised

C. That they will receive customer feedback

D. That they will go into General Availability

129. What can be a trade-off in improving a composite SLA by adding fallback mechanisms like a queue?

A. Simplified application logic

B. Reduced operational costs

C. Increased application complexity and costs

D. Decreased overall system resiliency

130. Why is it important to understand the Azure SLAs for products and services within your solution?
A. To ensure that Microsoft provides free upgrades
B. To help in creating achievable Application SLAs
C. To avoid legal action from Microsoft
D. To eliminate the need for disaster recovery planning

131. What is the primary function of an Azure account?
A. To provide free credits for all Microsoft services
B. To sign in to the Azure website and administer or deploy services
C. To offer community support forums exclusively
D. To act as a payment gateway for Microsoft products

132. What does an Azure subscription serve as in Microsoft Azure?
A. A database for storing user credentials
B. A logical container used to provision resources
C. A free credit system for all Microsoft services
D. An Azure AD replacement

133. What kind of relationship exists between an Azure subscription and Microsoft Entra ID (Azure AD)?
A. Competitive relationship
B. Trust relationship
C. Financial relationship
D. Legal relationship

134. How many Azure AD directories can a single Azure subscription trust?
A. Multiple directories
B. Only one directory
C. Two directories
D. No directories

135. What is included in every Azure subscription?
A. Exclusive access to Microsoft Office
B. Physical servers for deployment
C. Free access to billing, subscription support, and more
D. Unlimited credit for services

136. What does an Azure free subscription offer to new users?
A. Unlimited services for 12 months
B. $200 credit for the first 60 days
C. $200 credit for the first 30 days, free access to popular products for 12 months, and more
D. One-time access to Azure products

137. What is required to set up a free Azure subscription?
A. An Azure AD directory
B. A phone number, a credit card, and a Microsoft account
C. A subscription to Office 365
D. A special invitation from Microsoft

138. Who is the Azure Pay-As-You-Go (PAYG) subscription appropriate for?
A. Only individual users
B. Only large organizations
C. Only small businesses
D. A wide range of users, from individuals to large organizations

139. How are charges determined in an Azure Pay-As-You-Go subscription?
A. Fixed monthly charges
B. Prepaid credits
C. Monthly charges based on services used
D. Annual subscription fees

140. What does a user NOT need to provide when setting up an Azure PAYG subscription?
A. A phone number
B. A credit card
C. A Microsoft account
D. A $200 initial deposit

141. What is the purpose of the Pay-As-You-Go Dev/Test offer?
A. To provide a platform for gaming
B. To facilitate the purchase of hardware
C. To supply a cloud environment for development and testing
D. To offer a financial management service

142. Can you use the Pay-As-You-Go Dev/Test offer for production purposes?
A. Yes, for both production and development
B. No, it is limited to development and testing only
C. Yes, but with limited resources
D. No, it is exclusively for data storage

143. What does an Azure Enterprise Agreement offer?
A. A single-use license
B. Discounts on hardware purchases
C. Flexibility to buy cloud services and software licenses with discounts
D. A fixed pricing model for all Azure services

144. Who is eligible for the Azure for Students subscription?
A. Any individual with a student ID
B. Students with a verified organizational email address
C. All teachers and educators
D. Anyone with a valid credit card

145. What do you receive with an Azure for Students subscription?
A. $50 in Azure credits and free services with a credit card
B. A free laptop for educational purposes
C. $100 in Azure credits and select free services without needing a credit card
D. Unlimited access to all Azure services

146. Is a financially-backed SLA included in the Pay-As-You-Go Dev/Test subscription?
A. Yes, for all services
B. No, except for Visual Studio Team Services and HockeyApp
C. Yes, but only for storage services
D. No, SLAs are not available for any services

147. Can you create multiple Azure subscriptions under a single Azure account?
A. No, only one subscription is allowed per account
B. Yes, but only for personal use
C. Yes, and it's useful for businesses
D. No, you must create a new account for each subscription

148. What is the benefit of having multiple Azure subscriptions?
A. Increased computational power
B. Enhanced security protocols
C. Isolated environments and separate billing for different projects or teams
D. Unlimited data storage

149. What is required to sign up for an Azure for Students subscription?
A. A detailed project proposal
B. Parental consent
C. Verification of student status
D. A long-term commitment to Azure services

150. Under the Pay-As-You-Go Dev/Test offer, which Azure services are offered at low rates?
A. Virtual machines, Cloud Services, SQL Database, HDInsight, App Service, and Logic Apps
B. Office 365, SharePoint, and Exchange Server
C. Microsoft Entra ID and Windows Server
D. Dynamics 365 and Power BI

151. What does each Azure subscription generate on a monthly basis?
A. A detailed usage report
B. A bill
C. An activity summary
D. A performance review

152. How does Microsoft Entra ID (Azure AD) differ from Windows Active Directory?
A. Azure AD is for web-based authentication, while Windows AD is for desktops and servers
B. Azure AD is for desktops and servers, while Windows AD is for web-based authentication
C. There is no difference; they are the same
D. Azure AD is a payment system, while Windows AD is for authentication

153. What is a tenant in Microsoft Entra ID (Azure AD)?
A. A subscription plan for Azure services

B. A dedicated, isolated instance of the Microsoft Entra ID service

C. The original Azure account is responsible for billing

D. A user or application registered in Azure AD

154. Can a tenant be associated with multiple Azure subscriptions?

A. No, a tenant can be linked to only one Azure subscription

B. Yes, but only if the subscriptions are for the same department

C. Yes, a tenant can be associated with multiple Azure subscriptions

D. No, each tenant must be part of a separate Azure account

155. What happens if you sign up for Azure with an email address not associated with an existing tenant?

A. You cannot sign up without an existing tenant

B. Azure will automatically create a new tenant for you

C. The email address will be rejected

D. You will be prompted to join an existing tenant

156. What can you do to manage your spending on Azure?

A. Request a discount every month

B. Set spending limits on each subscription

C. Only use free services

D. Pay in a different currency

157. What does the line item say on your credit card statement for an Azure subscription charge?

A. Azure Service Charge

B. Cloud Service Fee

C. MSFT Azure

D. Microsoft Online Services

158. What is the relationship between Azure AD tenants and subscriptions?
A. One-to-many: one tenant can only have one subscription
B. Many-to-one: a tenant can have multiple subscriptions
C. Many-to-many: tenants and subscriptions can be interchangeably linked
D. One-to-one: each tenant is linked to one subscription, and vice versa

159. How can reports be generated in Azure if you have multiple internal departments?
A. By creating a single subscription for all departments
B. By creating individual user accounts for each department head
C. By creating separate subscriptions by department or project
D. Reports cannot be generated for multiple departments

160. Who is the account owner of an Azure AD tenant?
A. The user with the highest privileges
B. The original Azure account that is responsible for billing
C. The most recently added user
D. The designated IT department head

161. What is the initial response time for high-severity support requests under the Azure ProDirect support plan?
A. < 15 minutes
B. < 1 hour
C. < 2 hours
D. < 8 hours

162. Which Azure support plan assigns a Technical Account Manager to the account?
A. Developer
B. Standard

C. Professional Direct

D. Premier

163. What is the maximum severity for incidents under the Azure Developer support plan?

A. "A" (Critical business impact)

B. "B" (Moderate business impact)

C. "C" (Minimal business impact)

D. There is no severity level for the Developer plan

164. Which Azure support plan includes advisory services for operations and risk assessments?

A. Developer

B. Standard

C. Professional Direct

D. Premier

165. For which Azure support plan is the Developer support not available?

A. Standard

B. Professional Direct

C. Premier

D. Enterprise customers

166. How are support plans charged if purchased within a pay-as-you-go subscription?

A. An annual fee

B. Part of an Enterprise Agreement (EA)

C. A separate invoice

D. Charged to the monthly Azure subscription bill

167. What type of support is provided by the Azure Standard support plan for non-Microsoft technologies running on Azure?
A. No support
B. Only during business hours
C. Full support with assigned experts
D. Guidance and troubleshooting

168. Under which support plan can customers access the "Ask the Experts" webinars?
A. Developer
B. Standard
C. Professional Direct
D. Premier

169. What is the availability of technical support under the Basic support plan for Microsoft Azure?
A. 24x7 via email and phone
B. Business hours only
C. Unlimited 24x7 support
D. No technical support available

170. How can one access preview features?
A. By purchasing a subscription
B. Through the preview features page
C. By contacting customer support
D. All preview features are automatically available

171. Which tool can be used to manage Azure resources via a Graphical User Interface (GUI)?
A. Azure PowerShell
B. Azure CLI

C. Azure mobile app

D. Azure portal

172. How can you automate repetitive tasks in Azure?

A. Using Azure portal

B. Through Azure mobile app

C. By creating administration scripts in Azure PowerShell or Azure CLI

D. By resizing tiles in the Azure portal

173. Which of the following is a web-based command-line interface for Azure?

A. Azure PowerShell

B. Azure portal

C. Azure Cloud Shell

D. Azure SDKs

174. What is the use of the 'New-AzureRmVM' command in Azure PowerShell?

A. To delete a virtual machine

B. To update a virtual machine

C. To create a virtual machine

D. To start a virtual machine

175. What must be done before issuing Azure-specific commands in Azure PowerShell?

A. Install the Azure mobile app

B. Sign in using the Azure portal

C. Install the Azure PowerShell module and sign in using Connect-AzureRMAccount

D. Customize the Azure portal dashboard

176. What is the Azure mobile app primarily used for?
A. Writing administration scripts
B. Monitoring and managing Azure resources from a mobile device
C. Accessing Azure Cloud Shell
D. Running PowerShell commands

177. Why might using the Azure portal be considered time-consuming and error-prone for complex tasks?
A. It cannot be accessed from a browser
B. It does not allow customization of the dashboard
C. It cannot automate repetitive tasks
D. It only supports mobile devices

178. What is the first step in using Azure PowerShell to manage Azure resources?
A. Launch the Azure mobile app
B. Access the Azure SDK
C. Launch PowerShell and install the Azure PowerShell module
D. Sign in to the Azure portal

179. What is the disadvantage of setting up multiple VMs through the Azure portal?
A. VMs cannot be set up in different regions
B. VMs created cannot use different operating systems
C. VMs have to be created one at a time, which is inefficient
D. The portal does not support VM creation

180. What feature does the Azure portal offer for a high-level overview of your Azure environment?
A. Command parsing

B. A dashboard view
C. Mobile device management
D. Azure Cloud Shell access

181. What is the primary function of the Azure CLI?
A. To create graphical interfaces for Azure resources
B. To connect to Azure and execute administrative commands on Azure resources
C. To provide email support for Azure issues
D. To monitor the performance of Azure VMs in real-time

182. Which operating systems is Azure CLI compatible with?
A. Windows only
B. Mac OS only
C. Cross-platform
D. Linux only

183. How can you create a virtual machine using the Azure CLI?
A. Using the command `az vm start`
B. Using the command `az vm create`
C. Through the Azure Portal only
D. With the `az create vm` command

184. What are the two shell environments supported by Azure Cloud Shell?
A. Python and JavaScript
B. Bash and PowerShell
C. CMD and Bash
D. PowerShell and Python

185. Where can you use the Azure Cloud Shell?
A. On-premises servers only
B. In the Azure Mobile App
C. Only within the Azure Portal
D. In a browser-based environment

186. What is Microsoft Entra ID (Azure AD) primarily used for?
A. Monitoring and managing Azure resources
B. Managing user identities and access
C. Storing relational databases
D. Hosting web applications

187. Which platforms does the Azure Mobile App support?
A. iOS only
B. Android only
C. Both iOS and Android
D. Windows Phone

188. What other options are available for managing Azure resources besides CLI and Cloud Shell?
A. Azure SDKs and REST APIs
B. Azure automated scripts only
C. Azure webhooks only.
D. Only third-party tools

189. What is the primary use of the Azure portal?
A. To read the documentation about Azure
B. To interact with subscriptions and resources created in Azure
C. To download Azure SDKs
D. To purchase Azure services

190. When creating a virtual machine, can you generate SSH keys using the Azure CLI?
A. No, SSH keys must be generated externally
B. Yes, with the parameter `--generate-ssh-keys.`
C. SSH keys are not used in Azure
D. Only through the Azure portal

191. What is the primary graphical user interface for controlling Microsoft Azure?
A. Azure Command Line Interface (CLI)
B. Azure Cloud Shell
C. Azure Management Console
D. Azure Portal

192. In the Azure portal, what term is used to describe a slide-out panel containing the UI for a single level in a navigation sequence?
A. Dashboard
B. Widget
C. Blade
D. Module

193. What can customers find in the Azure Marketplace?
A. Only Microsoft services
B. Social media plugins
C. Applications and services from service providers
D. Physical hardware for data centers

194. How many listings are available in the Azure Marketplace at the time of this writing?
A. Over 500 listings
B. Over 8,000 listings

C. Over 10,000 listings

D. Over 15,000 listings

195. Is it possible to test the next version of the Azure portal?

A. Yes, but only after GA

B. No, it is not available for testing

C. Yes, it is available for public preview

D. Yes, it is available in private preview only

196. Which service would you use to manage policies and compliance across multiple Azure subscriptions?

A. Azure Monitor

B. Azure Policy

C. Azure Resource Manager

D. Azure Advisor

197. Where can you access the Azure Cloud Shell in the Azure portal?

A. By clicking the 'Help & Support' button

B. By clicking the Cloud Shell icon (>_)

C. By selecting it from the 'All services' menu

D. By opening the 'Settings' panel

198. What categories does the Azure Marketplace solution catalog span?

A. Only cloud storage and databases

B. Only virtual machines and networking

C. Only security and developer tools

D. Multiple categories, including databases, security, and developer tools

199. What can customers do with the solutions and services found in the Azure Marketplace?

A. Only purchase them

B. Only provision them

C. Only review them

D. Discover, try, buy, or deploy them

200. What type of applications and services does Azure Marketplace offer?

A. Only SaaS applications

B. Only consulting services

C. Only virtual machines

D. SaaS applications, Virtual Machines, Solution Templates, Azure-Managed applications, and consulting services

201. What is Azure Compute primarily used for?

A. Permanent data storage

B. Running cloud-based applications

C. Email hosting services

D. Content delivery networks

202. Which of the following is NOT a common technique for performing computing in Azure?

A. Virtual machines

B. Containers

C. Azure App Service

D. Physical servers

203. What are virtual machines in the context of Azure Compute?

A. Physical computers hosted in Azure data centers

B. Software emulations of physical computers

C. Networking resources only

D. Storage services for large data sets

204. What is a distinctive feature of containers compared to virtual machines?

A. Containers require a separate operating system for each instance
B. Containers are not capable of running applications
C. Containers use the host operating system for running applications
D. Containers provide virtual networking resources only

205. What is Azure App Service best designed for?
A. Data analytics services
B. Hosting desktop applications
C. Hosting enterprise-grade web-oriented applications
D. Managing virtual networks

206. How does serverless computing work in Azure?
A. It requires users to manage the underlying hosting environment
B. It runs code without abstracting the underlying hosting environment
C. It abstracts the underlying hosting environment and runs your code
D. It's focused on virtual machine management

207. What is the primary function of Azure Resource Manager (ARM)?
A. To automate the deployment of Azure resources
B. To manage Azure subscriptions and billing
C. To provide secure communication between Azure and on-premises networks
D. To monitor the performance and health of Azure resources

208. Which Azure service allows you to use a remote desktop client?
A. Azure App Service
B. Containers
C. Serverless computing
D. Virtual machines

209. In Azure, what are containers typically used for?
A. Running applications with heavy dependency on external libraries

B. Running applications without the need for an embedded operating system

C. Storing large volumes of data

D. Providing physical networking solutions

210. Which Azure service is designed for storing large amounts of unstructured data such as text or binary data?
A. Azure SQL Database
B. Azure Blob Storage
C. Azure Virtual Machines
D. Microsoft Entra ID

211. What is Azure Virtual Machines (VM) primarily used for?
A. Web hosting
B. Virtualized server infrastructure
C. Data analysis
D. Machine learning

212. What type of service does Azure VMs offer?
A. Platform as a Service (PaaS)
B. Software as a Service (SaaS)
C. Infrastructure as a Service (IaaS)
D. Database as a Service (DBaaS)

213. Which of the following is NOT a reason to use Azure VMs?
A. To gain total control over the hardware
B. To run custom software
C. To use custom hosting configurations
D. To have total control over the operating system

214. What can you customize on an Azure VM?
A. The physical server location
B. The cloud service provider
C. The software running on the VM
D. The internet speed of the VM

215. How quickly can you create and provision a VM in Azure?
A. Within a few days
B. In minutes
C. In several hours
D. Instantaneously

216. What is a VM image in Azure?
A. A backup of a VM
B. A template used to create a VM
C. A virtual hard disk
D. A snapshot of a VM at a point in time

217. When creating a VM in Azure, why is selecting an image important?
A. It determines the geographic location of the VM
B. It affects the VM's performance
C. It dictates the pre-configured operating system and software
D. It sets the pricing for the VM

218. What is an ideal choice for needing total control over an operating system in the cloud?
A. Azure Web Apps
B. Azure Blob Storage
C. Azure Virtual Machines
D. Azure Functions

219. What can Azure VMs be used for besides providing total control over the OS?
A. Only for data storage
B. Only for email hosting
C. Running custom software and custom hosting configurations
D. Only for network infrastructure

220. What does selecting a pre-configured VM image in Azure help you bypass?
A. The need to manually install the OS
B. The necessity to create a VM from scratch
C. The requirement for physical hardware
D. All of the above

221. What is the primary purpose of an Availability Set in Azure?
A. To group identical VMs for load balancing
B. To provide a logical grouping of VMs for high-availability
C. To automatically scale VMs based on the demand
D. To patch security vulnerabilities within VMs

222. How many fault domains can you get with an Availability Set?
A. One
B. Two
C. Three
D. Five

223. What is the purpose of updating domains in an Availability Set?
A. To ensure VMs are updated to the latest OS version
B. To provide backup services for VMs
C. To group VMs that will be rebooted together
D. To enable automatic scaling of VMs

224. What kind of maintenance event would involve a hardware failure in the data center?
A. Planned maintenance event
B. Unplanned maintenance event
C. Routine maintenance event
D. Scheduled maintenance event

225. How many logical update domains are available within an Availability Set?
A. Two
B. Three
C. Four
D. Five

226. What are Virtual Machine Scale Sets used for in Azure?
A. To manage a single VM
B. To create a logical group for high-availability
C. To manage a group of identical, load-balanced VMs
D. To provide physical separation of VMs

227. If you need to automatically balance traffic and distribute it across multiple VM instances, which service should you use?
A. Availability Set
B. Azure Batch
C. Virtual Machine Scale Set
D. Azure Automation

228. What is the cost implication of using Virtual Machine Scale Sets for the management and automation features they provide?
A. Additional charges for auto-scale and redundancy
B. No additional cost for the management and automation features

C. A one-time setup fee for the scale set

D. Monthly subscription fees for scale set features

229. Which feature should be used to automatically distribute VM instances across Availability Zones or Availability Sets?

A. Azure Load Balancer

B. Azure Automation

C. Virtual Machine Scale Sets

D. Azure Batch

230. What do you need to do to add additional VM instances in a manual group of VMs compared to using Virtual Machine Scale Sets?

A. Manually create an Availability Set

B. Automatically create from a central configuration

C. Use Azure Batch for scaling

D. Manual process to create, configure, and ensure compliance

231. What is the primary function of Azure Batch?

A. Web hosting

B. Email services

C. Job scheduling and compute management

D. Database management

232. Which feature is NOT a part of Azure Batch capabilities?

A. Automatic scaling of VMs

B. Email server configuration

C. Identification of failures

D. Re-queuing of work

233. How can containers be beneficial in a virtual machine environment?
A. They require more storage space than VMs
B. They can only run one instance of an application per VM
C. They allow multiple isolated applications to run on a single VM host
D. They are less secure than traditional VMs

234. What Azure service offers the simplest way to run a container?
A. Azure Virtual Machines
B. Azure Container Instances (ACI)
C. Azure Blob Storage
D. Azure Functions

235. What is the role of Azure Kubernetes Service (AKS)?
A. It is a web hosting service.
B. It is a file storage service.
C. It is an email automation service.
D. It is an orchestration service for containers.

236. What are the main ways to manage containers in Azure?
A. Azure Container Instances and Azure Kubernetes Service
B. Azure Functions and Azure Logic Apps
C. Azure Virtual Network and Azure ExpressRoute
D. Azure SQL Database and Azure Cosmos DB

237. What architectural approach do containers support well?
A. Monolithic architecture
B. Micro-service architecture
C. Single-tier architecture
D. Big data architecture

238. In a micro-service architecture, how might a website be containerized?
A. Using a single container for the entire website
B. Splitting the website into front end, back end, and storage containers
C. Using a separate VM for each part of the website
D. Storing the entire website in a single blob storage container

239. Which Azure service is a PaaS offering for running containers without managing VMs?
A. Azure App Service
B. Microsoft Entra ID
C. Azure Container Instances (ACI)
D. Azure Virtual Network

240. What is the purpose of container orchestration in Azure?
A. To manage hardware devices
B. To coordinate and automate container deployment, management, and scaling
C. To facilitate software installation on VMs
D. To provide data encryption services

241. What is the primary advantage of using containers for running multiple instances of an application on Azure?
A. Higher costs for better performance
B. Running a single application per virtual machine
C. Lightweight and dynamic scalability
D. Containers require additional VMs for isolation

242. Which Azure service provides a platform for building, deploying, and managing applications without dealing with the underlying infrastructure?
A. Azure Virtual Machines
B. Azure Functions

C. Azure App Service
D. Azure Kubernetes Service

243. What is the purpose of Azure Kubernetes Service (AKS)?
A. To provide a managed virtual machine service
B. To offer a simple file storage solution
C. To serve as a complete orchestration service for containers
D. To facilitate static website hosting

244. In a micro-service architecture, how might containers be utilized?
A. By combining all services into a single large container
B. By running the database alone in a dedicated container
C. By splitting a solution into smaller, independent containers
D. By avoiding the use of containers for simplified management

245. What is Azure App Service primarily used for?
A. Data analysis and machine learning tasks
B. Building and hosting web apps and related services
C. Container orchestration
D. Storing unstructured data blobs

246. Which programming languages are supported by the Azure App Service for hosting web apps?
A. Only .NET and .NET Core
B. Only Java and Python
C. Only Ruby and Node.js
D. ASP.NET, Java, Ruby, Node.js, PHP, and Python

247. What is the key feature of Azure API Apps?
A. Providing virtual desktops
B. Building REST-based Web APIs with full Swagger support

C. Email hosting services

D. Blockchain as a Service

248. What are WebJobs in Azure App Service used for?

A. Real-time data streaming

B. Running background tasks within the same context as web apps

C. Hosting static websites

D. Processing large volumes of data in big data scenarios

249. Which operating systems can you choose for hosting web apps on Azure App Service?

A. Windows only

B. Linux only

C. Both Windows and Linux

D. macOS only

250. What aspect of infrastructure management is handled by Azure App Service?

A. Networking equipment maintenance

B. Physical server hardware upgrades

C. Deployment and management of web apps

D. Installation of on-premises databases

251. What feature of Azure App Service helps you quickly build a back-end for iOS and Android apps?

A. Azure Functions

B. Azure Logic Apps

C. Mobile Apps

D. Azure SQL Database

252. What can Azure Functions execute?
A. Logic workflows only
B. Code in almost any modern language
C. Visual designer workflows
D. Business process automation

253. How does Azure's serverless computing bill you?
A. Fixed monthly rate
B. Per user subscription
C. For the exact resources you use
D. Annual subscription

254. What are Azure Durable Functions?
A. Stateless Azure Functions
B. Azure Logic Apps
C. Stateful Azure Functions
D. The visual designer in Azure

255. What are Azure Logic Apps specifically designed to automate?
A. Code deployment
B. Server management
C. Business processes
D. Data storage

256. Which Azure service provides over 200 different connectors and processing blocks to interact with different services?
A. Azure Functions
B. Azure Mobile Apps
C. Azure Logic Apps
D. Azure SQL Database

257. How can you create workflows in Azure Logic Apps?
A. Using a command-line interface
B. Through a visual designer on the Azure Portal or in Visual Studio
C. By writing extensive code in C# or Node.js
D. With a physical workflow diagram

258. What is the default behavior of Azure Functions in terms of state management?
A. Stateful
B. Stateless
C. Hybrid state management
D. Persistent state

259. What is the trigger for serverless apps in Azure to run?
A. A fixed schedule
B. Manual intervention
C. An event
D. A specific user request

260. What can you do with the Mobile Apps feature of Azure App Service?
A. Execute custom back-end logic in C# or Node.js
B. Authenticate customers with enterprise accounts only
C. Send emails to users
D. Manage virtual machines

261. What is the primary function of Azure Event Grid?
A. Data analytics
B. Event-driven reactive programming

C. Data storage
D. Resource monitoring

262. Which Azure service is best suited for big data pipeline scenarios?
A. Azure Event Grid
B. Azure Functions
C. Azure Service Bus
D. Azure Event Hubs

263. When should you use Azure Service Bus?
A. For telemetry and distributed data streaming
B. For high-value enterprise messaging that requires transactions and ordering
C. To react to status changes within your resources
D. For developing stateless applications

264. Which of the following is NOT a concept in Azure Event Grid?
A. Event subscriptions
B. Event handlers
C. Event loops
D. Event sources

265. What is a key feature of Durable Functions in Azure Functions?
A. They provide a GUI for action definitions
B. They run exclusively in the cloud
C. They provide stateful functions
D. They support big data pipelines

266. Which Azure service would you use to store and manage secrets, such as API keys and passwords?

A. Azure Storage
B. Azure Key Vault
C. Azure SQL Database
D. Microsoft Entra ID

267. What development approach does Azure Logic Apps use?
A. Code-first (imperative)
B. Designer-first (declarative)
C. Command-line interface
D. Local server deployment

268. What kind of execution context does Azure Functions support?
A. Only in the cloud
B. Only on local servers
C. Both locally and in the cloud
D. None, it's not executable

269. In Azure Event Grid, what is the purpose of event subscriptions?
A. To handle the execution of functions
B. To provide a GUI for users
C. To route events to the appropriate event handler
D. To store messages in a broker

270. If you need to ensure reliable state transition management for business processes, which Azure service should you choose?
A. Azure Event Grid
B. Azure Event Hubs
C. Azure Service Bus
D. Azure Functions

271. What is the primary purpose of Azure IoT solutions?
A. To provide web hosting services
B. To connect, monitor, and control IoT assets
C. To offer online gaming platforms
D. To facilitate email communication services

272. Which of the following is NOT a component of an IoT solution in Azure?
A. Devices
B. Back-end services
C. Communication networks
D. Mobile applications

273. What is the function of Azure IoT Central?
A. It is a PaaS solution for web hosting
B. It is a SaaS solution for connecting, monitoring, and managing IoT devices
C. It is a database service for IoT devices
D. It is a messaging service for IoT communications

274. What are IoT solution accelerators primarily used for?
A. To slow down IoT development for better quality control
B. To provide templates and accelerate the development of an IoT solution
C. To manage financial transactions in IoT devices
D. To offer entertainment services through IoT

275. Which service in Azure IoT enables the creation of comprehensive models of the physical environment?
A. IoT Central
B. IoT Hub
C. Azure Digital Twins
D. Time Series Insights

276. What is the purpose of the IoT Hub Device Provisioning Service?
A. It provides email services for IoT devices
B. It is used to secure and rapidly provision devices to an IoT hub
C. It is utilized for creating mobile applications
D. It is a data visualization tool for IoT devices

277. What is the benefit of using IoT Edge?
A. It increases the amount of data sent to the cloud
B. It allows for data analysis on the devices themselves, reducing cloud communication
C. It is a gaming platform for IoT devices
D. It provides GPS services for IoT devices

278. What does Azure Maps offer to IoT solutions?
A. Cryptocurrency mining tools
B. Geographic information and mapping capabilities
C. Email marketing services
D. Social media analytics

279. In the context of Azure IoT, what could a back-end service ask a device to do?
A. Play a video game
B. Send temperature telemetry more frequently to help diagnose a problem
C. Make a phone call
D. Perform a web search

280. Which Azure service helps in storing, visualizing, and querying large amounts of time series data from IoT devices?
A. Microsoft Entra ID
B. Time Series Insights

C. Azure Blob Storage

D. Azure Virtual Machines

281. What is Azure IoT Central primarily used for?

A. Managing cloud storage solutions

B. Creating connected product experiences

C. Offering web hosting services

D. Developing mobile applications

282. Which feature is NOT provided by Azure IoT Solution Accelerators?

A. Remote monitoring

B. Predictive maintenance

C. Connected factory

D. Mobile app development

283. What is the key purpose of Azure IoT Hub?

A. To provide a database management system

B. To act as a central message hub for IoT device communication

C. To host web applications

D. To offer machine learning capabilities

284. Which of the following is a capability of Azure Stream Analytics?

A. Managing IoT devices

B. Analyzing real-time telemetry streams from IoT devices

C. Provisioning new user accounts

D. Storing static website content

285. What are the primary communication patterns supported by IoT Hub?

A. Email and chat services

B. File upload and social media feeds

C. Device-to-cloud telemetry and cloud-to-device messages

D. Video streaming and content delivery

286. What is Azure IoT Edge designed for?
A. Enhancing cloud storage options
B. Moving workloads to the edge for localized device data analysis
C. Providing email server functionality
D. Developing desktop applications

287. Which Azure service helps to model the relationships and interactions between people, spaces, and devices?
A. Azure Virtual Machines
B. Azure Digital Twins
C. Azure Blob Storage
D. Azure Functions

288. What is the purpose of the IoT Hub Device Provisioning Service?
A. It serves as a messaging app for IoT devices
B. It supports zero-touch, just-in-time provisioning to the correct IoT hub
C. It is a payment gateway for IoT devices
D. It enables direct file storage from IoT devices

289. What differentiates the Basic and Standard tiers of IoT Hub?
A. The Basic tier supports device management, while the Standard tier does not
B. The Standard tier supports cloud-to-device messaging, while the Basic tier does not
C. The Basic tier offers enterprise-grade security, while the Standard tier does not
D. The Standard tier supports device simulation, while the Basic tier does not

290. Which service does Azure IoT Central use to customize applications?
A. Azure Machine Learning

B. Microsoft Entra ID

C. Azure IoT Hub

D. Azure SQL Database

291. What is the primary function of Azure Time Series Insights?

A. To provide virtual reality experiences

B. To manage and analyze social media data

C. To store, visualize, and query large amounts of time series data

D. To offer cloud gaming services

292. Which service offers geographic information for web and mobile applications?

A. Azure Functions

B. Azure Maps

C. Microsoft Entra ID

D. Azure Cosmos DB

293. What is the purpose of machine learning, as described in the Azure Fundamentals?

A. To enable remote control of devices

B. To facilitate online payments

C. To forecast future behaviors, outcomes, and trends using data

D. To provide cybersecurity services

294. What does Azure Machine Learning service support for building machine learning models?

A. Only proprietary Microsoft technologies

B. Only classical machine learning techniques

C. Open-source technologies like PyTorch, TensorFlow, and sci-kit-learn

D. Exclusive support for deep learning models

295. How does Azure Machine Learning Studio allow users to build predictive analysis models?
A. By writing complex code only
B. By using a command-line interface
C. Using an interactive, visual workspace with drag-and-drop functionality
D. By outsourcing model development to Azure's data science team

296. What is the key difference between Azure Machine Learning Studio and Azure Machine Learning service?
A. Machine Learning Studio requires code for model building; the service does not
B. Machine Learning Studio uses proprietary compute targets; the service uses your own compute resources
C. Machine Learning Studio is not integrated into Azure; the service is
D. Machine Learning Studio is optimized for Apache Spark; the service is not

297. Which compute targets does Azure Machine Learning Studio support for training?
A. GPU and TPU support only
B. Proprietary compute target with CPU support only
C. User's own compute resources
D. Cloud-based virtual machines only

298. Can you perform automated model training and hyper-parameter tuning in Azure Machine Learning Studio?
A. Yes, it's fully supported
B. Yes, but only for certain models
C. No, this feature is not available
D. No, but it's available in the visual interface

299. What is Azure Databricks optimized for?
A. Real-time communication services
B. Apache Spark-based analytics on the Microsoft Azure cloud services platform
C. Gaming and multimedia processing
D. Blockchain technologies

300. Which services can Azure Databricks read data from for analytics?
A. Azure Blob Storage, Azure Data Lake Storage, Azure Cosmos DB, and Azure SQL Data Warehouse
B. Azure Maps and IoT Hub only
C. Microsoft Entra ID and Azure Functions
D. Azure Virtual Machines and Azure Kubernetes Service

301. What is one of the primary benefits of Azure data storage when it comes to data security?
A. Unlimited data storage
B. Automated marketing tools
C. Encryption capabilities
D. Free data storage solutions

302. Azure data storage can handle which of the following types of data?
A. Only text files
B. Only video files
C. Only NoSQL data
D. Multiple data types

303. How much data can Azure's virtual disks store?
A. Up to 2 TB
B. Up to 4 TB
C. Up to 6 TB

D. Up to 8 TB

304. What does Azure use to prioritize access to data based on usage frequency?
A. Data analytics
B. Storage tiers
C. Virtual disks
D. Encryption

305. What is structured data in Azure Storage?
A. Data that adheres to a schema with unrestricted formats
B. Data without any designated structure
C. Data that adheres to a schema with the same fields or properties
D. Data organized using tags or keys.

306. What are the replication capabilities of Azure data storage intended to protect against?
A. Unauthorized data access
B. Data replication errors
C. Planned or unplanned events
D. Data analytics performance issues

307. Which type of data uses tags or keys to organize and provide hierarchy?
A. Structured data
B. Unstructured data
C. Semi-structured data
D. Encrypted data

308. What can unstructured data include?
A. Only JSON files

B. Only PDF documents

C. Only relational tables

D. Various formats like PDFs, images, JSON files, and video content

309. What is a significant feature of Azure data storage for disaster recovery?

A. Data sharing

B. Automated backup and recovery

C. Data analysis tools

D. Data input simplification

310. What kind of data relies on keys to indicate relationships between rows in different tables?

A. Semi-structured data

B. Unstructured data

C. Structured data

D. Encrypted data

311. What is Azure SQL Database?

A. A file storage service

B. A NoSQL database service

C. A relational database as a service (DaaS)

D. A web hosting service

312. Which service does Azure Database Migration Service use to generate assessment reports?

A. Azure Analysis Services

B. Data Migration Assistant

C. Azure Data Factory

D. Azure Synapse Analytics

313. What type of processing does Azure SQL Data Warehouse use?
A. Single-threaded processing
B. Dual-threaded processing
C. Massively Parallel Processing (MPP)
D. Sequential processing

314. What is the role of SQL Data Warehouse in a big data solution?
A. To store unstructured data
B. To act as a key component for running high-performance analytics
C. To serve as a transactional database
D. To provide real-time streaming capabilities

315. How does SQL Data Warehouse integrate big data for analysis?
A. Through RESTful APIs
B. By using PolyBase T-SQL queries
C. With direct file uploads
D. Via streaming data ingestion

316. What is the storage format used by SQL Data Warehouse to reduce costs and improve query performance?
A. Row-based storage
B. XML storage
C. Columnar storage
D. JSON storage

317. What is the outcome of running analytics on SQL Data Warehouse?
A. Data visualization
B. Single version of truth for business insights
C. Real-time data streaming
D. Data encryption

318. What is the typical performance improvement for analysis queries when using SQL Data Warehouse compared to traditional database systems?
A. Queries finish at the same time
B. Queries take slightly less time
C. Queries finish in seconds instead of minutes or hours instead of days
D. There is no performance improvement

319. Where can the analysis results from SQL Data Warehouse be directed?
A. Only to data lakes
B. To worldwide reporting databases or applications
C. Solely to on-premises servers
D. Exclusively to mobile applications

320. What is the key benefit of using SQL Data Warehouse for business analysts?
A. To improve data entry processes
B. To gain insights into making well-informed business decisions
C. To automate customer service interactions
D. To enhance social media presence

321. What is Azure Cosmos DB?
A. Microsoft's globally distributed, multi-model database service
B. A local database service for small-scale applications
C. Microsoft's cloud storage solution for modern data storage scenarios
D. A messaging service for inter-application communication

322. What kinds of data models does Azure Cosmos DB support?
A. Only SQL
B. SQL, MongoDB, Cassandra, Tables, and Gremlin

C. Only NoSQL

D. Only MongoDB and Gremlin

323. What is Azure Storage primarily used for?

A. Data analysis and machine learning

B. Modern data storage scenarios

C. Database management exclusively

D. Web hosting services

324. Which Azure Storage service is optimized for storing massive amounts of unstructured data?

A. Azure Tables

B. Azure Files

C. Azure Queues

D. Azure Blobs

325. How can users and client applications access objects in Azure Blob storage?

A. Only via Azure Storage REST API

B. Via HTTP/HTTPS from anywhere in the world

C. Only through Azure PowerShell

D. Exclusively with Azure CLI

326. Which programming languages are supported by Azure Storage client libraries?

A. Only .NET and Java

B. C++, Python, and Swift

C. .NET, Java, Node.js, Python, Go, PHP, and Ruby

D. Only PHP and Ruby

327. What is the primary use case for Azure Queues?

A. Data backup and restore

B. Reliable messaging between application components

C. Object storage for large text files
D. Structured NoSQL storage

328. What is the purpose of Azure Tables within Azure Storage?
A. To provide a relational database
B. For structured NoSQL storage
C. To store binary data
D. To facilitate web hosting

329. How does Azure Cosmos DB ensure low latency and high availability?
A. By deploying instances in a single data center
B. Through a fixed global distribution
C. By deploying instances in data centers close to users
D. Through single-region deployment

330. What can Azure Blob Storage be used for? (Choose all that apply)
A. Storing data for backup and restore
B. Relational database management
C. Streaming video and audio
D. Messaging between application components

331. What is the primary purpose of Azure Data Lake Storage Gen2?
A. To provide a relational database management system
B. To offer a messaging service for cloud applications
C. To build enterprise data lakes on Azure
D. To serve as a primary storage for virtual machines

332. How are data lakes different from data warehouses?
A. Data lakes are for structured data only, while data warehouses are for unstructured data
B. Data lakes store raw data without a defined purpose, whereas data

warehouses store processed data for a specific purpose

C. Data warehouses have a larger storage capacity than data lakes

D. Data lakes are less secure than data warehouses

333. What significant feature does Data Lake Storage Gen2 include that enhances data organization?

A. Hierarchical namespace

B. Relational data model

C. Object-based storage exclusivity

D. Data encryption

334. Which of the following operations becomes more efficient with the hierarchical namespace in Data Lake Storage Gen2?

A. Data encryption

B. Data replication

C. Renaming or deleting a directory

D. Generating relational database schemas

335. Which tools are recommended for running data analysis jobs on data stored in Data Lake Storage Gen2?

A. Azure Functions and Azure Logic Apps

B. Azure HDInsight and Azure Databricks

C. Azure Machine Learning and Azure Cognitive Services

D. Azure SQL Database and Azure Synapse Analytics

336. What is Azure Data Lake Analytics?

A. A data warehousing service

B. An on-demand analytics job service

C. A real-time data streaming service

D. A machine learning service

337. How does Azure HDInsight support big data processing?
A. By offering a managed NoSQL database
B. By providing a managed, full-spectrum, open-source analytics service
C. By serving as a content delivery network
D. By enabling data caching and CDN services

338. What analogy is used to describe Azure Data Lake?
A. A library with a cataloging system
B. A large container like a real lake with rivers flowing into it
C. A secure vault for valuable data assets
D. A cloud-based spreadsheet for structured data

339. What types of data can Azure Data Lake store?
A. Only structured data such as databases
B. Only unstructured data, such as images and videos
C. Only real-time data streams
D. Structured data, unstructured data, log files, real-time data, images, etc.

340. What is Azure HDInsight primarily used for?
A. Building and deploying web applications
B. Processing massive amounts of data through services like Hadoop or Spark
C. Hosting virtual machines and containers
D. Managing identity and access for Azure services

341. What protocol does Azure Files use to allow file access?
A. FTP
B. HTTP
C. SMB
D. NFS

342. How can Azure Files be accessed from anywhere in the world?
A. Via a direct server connection
B. By using a URL with a SAS token
C. Through a VPN
D. Only through Azure portal

343. What is a common scenario for using Azure Files?
A. Hosting websites
B. Migrating on-premises applications that share data with Azure
C. Streaming videos
D. Running high-performance computing tasks

344. What is Azure Queue Storage primarily used for?
A. Storing persistent files
B. Storing large numbers of messages
C. Hosting databases
D. Saving configuration settings

345. What benefit does Azure Queue Storage offer for web servers?
A. Static website hosting
B. Increased storage capacity
C. Asynchronous message queueing
D. Real-time data processing

346. What type of storage object is an Azure-managed disk stored as?
A. Block blob
B. Queue
C. Page blob
D. Table

347. What does the term 'managed' signify in the context of Azure-managed disks?
A. User has to manage everything manually
B. Azure automates underlying storage account management
C. Third-party services manage disks
D. Disks require manual scaling

348. What is a typical use case for Azure Disk Storage?
A. Temporary data caching
B. Data archiving
C. Persistent data storage for VMs
D. Message queueing

349. Can Azure Files be used for storing and accessing configuration files from multiple VMs?
A. Yes
B. No
C. Only if the files are read-only
D. Only through the REST interface

350. What is the benefit of decoupling application components using Azure Queue Storage?
A. Reducing storage costs
B. Increased application security
C. Building resilience against component failure
D. Simplifying database management

351. What is the primary use case for Azure Table storage?
A. Storing files for frequent access
B. Hosting web applications
C. Storing structured NoSQL data
D. Running big data analytics

352. What protocol and query language can be used to access data in Azure Table storage?
A. SQL and JDBC
B. OData protocol and LINQ queries
C. FTP and regular expressions
D. REST API and Python

353. When should you consider using Azure Blobs?
A. When you need to store persistent data for virtual machines
B. When your application uses native file system APIs
C. When you want to perform big data analytics
D. When you require a traditional SQL database

354. What feature does Azure Files provide that is particularly useful for "lift and shift" scenarios?
A. A NoSQL database
B. An SMB interface for file access
C. A virtual hard disk
D. An archive storage tier

355. Which Azure storage feature is optimized for data that is accessed frequently?
A. Archive storage tier
B. Cool storage tier
C. Hot storage tier
D. Azure Disks

356. What is the minimum storage duration recommended for data in the Azure cool access tier?
A. 7 days
B. 30 days

C. 180 days

D. 1 year

357. Which of the following operations are valid for blobs in the Azure archive access tier?

A. Read and write operations

B. GetBlobProperties and DeleteBlob

C. Snapshot creation

D. Immediate data retrieval

358. Which encryption type in Azure provides security for data at rest?

A. Client-side encryption

B. Microsoft Entra ID Encryption

C. Azure Storage Service Encryption (SSE)

D. Transport Layer Security (TLS)

359. What is the term used to describe the process of ensuring data is durable and always available in Azure?

A. Data redundancy

B. Data replication

C. Data encryption

D. Data tiering

360. For which scenario is the Azure Disk storage most appropriate?

A. Storing data that needs to be accessed from outside the virtual machine

B. Lift and shift applications that use file system APIs for data access

C. Storing data that requires complex joins and foreign keys

D. Building an enterprise data lake for analytics

361. What is the purpose of Azure Virtual Network (VNet)?

A. To provide a content delivery network (CDN)

B. To enable Azure resources to securely communicate with each other, the

internet, and on-premises networks
C. To host DNS domains outside the Microsoft Azure infrastructure
D. To monitor network resources in Azure

362. What is Azure ExpressRoute primarily used for?
A. To send encrypted traffic over the public Internet
B. To extend on-premises networks into the Microsoft cloud over a private connection facilitated by a connectivity provider
C. To optimize and automate branch connectivity in Azure
D. To provide DDoS protection services

363. Which Azure service offers optimized and automated branch connectivity to and through Azure?
A. Virtual Network (VNet)
B. VPN Gateway
C. Virtual WAN
D. Azure Bastion

364. How can virtual networks (VNets) be connected?
A. Using Azure DNS
B. Through Azure Bastion
C. By assigning public IP addresses
D. Using virtual network peering

365. What is the function of Azure DNS?
A. To provide VPN connectivity
B. To protect against DDoS attacks
C. To host DNS domains that provide name resolution using Microsoft Azure infrastructure
D. To facilitate content delivery using CDN

366. What is the advantage of using Azure Bastion?
A. It allows for DDoS protection
B. It enables secure and seamless RDP/SSH connectivity to virtual machines without a public IP address
C. It provides a private connection facilitated by a connectivity provider
D. It automates branch connectivity to Azure

367. In Azure Virtual Network, how can resources communicate inbound to the internet?
A. By using a private IP address
B. By assigning a public IP address or a public Load Balancer
C. Through Azure Virtual WAN
D. By leveraging Azure DNS

368. What service sends encrypted traffic between an Azure virtual network and an on-premises location over the public Internet?
A. Azure Front Door Service
B. VPN Gateway
C. Azure Bastion
D. Azure Monitor

369. For what purpose can you connect your on-premises computers and networks to a virtual network?
A. To host web applications
B. To use Azure as a CDN
C. To enable secure branch connectivity
D. To communicate with the virtual network

370. What does Azure Traffic Manager provide?
A. DNS hosting services
B. Secure and seamless RDP/SSH connectivity
C. DDoS protection and firewall
D. Application delivery services

371. What is the primary purpose of Azure DDoS protection?
A. To provide additional storage options for data
B. To ensure high availability for applications with protection from excess IP traffic
C. To monitor network performance and utilization
D. To manage web traffic across regional backend

372. Which Azure service offers global load balancing by optimizing for best performance and instant global failover for high availability?
A. Azure Front Door Service
B. Azure Load Balancer
C. Azure Traffic Manager
D. Azure Application Gateway

373. What is the role of Azure Firewall?
A. To store cached content on edge servers
B. To provide global routing for web traffic
C. To protect Azure Virtual Network resources with a managed network security service
D. To distribute traffic across availability zones

374. Which service is responsible for providing internal load-balancing within Azure virtual networks (VNets)?
A. Traffic Manager
B. Azure Front Door Service
C. Azure Load Balancer
D. Azure Application Gateway

375. What does Azure Traffic Manager use to redirect web traffic requests to the most appropriate geographical location endpoint?

A. Packet inspection
B. HTTP routing rules
C. DNS
D. Edge servers

376. What is the benefit of using an N-tier architecture for an e-commerce web application?
A. To consolidate all services into a single tier for simplicity
B. To ensure that higher tiers can never access services from lower tiers
C. To allow for independent updates or replacements of tiers
D. To use a single data center for the entire application

377. What is the function of Azure Application Gateway?
A. To monitor and troubleshoot connectivity issues
B. To act as a web traffic load balancer and manage traffic to web applications
C. To provide high availability for applications with protection from excess IP traffic
D. To deliver high-bandwidth content to users with minimal latency

378. Which Azure service helps monitor and troubleshoot connectivity issues on your VMs?
A. Azure Monitor
B. Azure Front Door Service
C. Network Watcher
D. ExpressRoute Monitor

379. What is the role of Azure's Content Delivery Network (CDN)?
A. To provide global routing for web traffic
B. To distribute traffic across global Azure regions
C. To deliver high-bandwidth content to users with minimal latency
D. To protect against distributed denial-of-service attacks

380. What is an Azure Region?
A. A specific service within Azure for regional load balancing
B. A managed group of virtual machines within a single data center
C. One or more Azure data centers within a specific geographic location
D. A network security group within Azure

381. What is a virtual network in Azure?
A. A physical network infrastructure within Azure data centers
B. A single, global network that spans all Azure regions
C. A logically isolated network within a single Azure region
D. A third-party networking service integrated with Azure

382. How can multiple virtual networks from different regions be connected?
A. By using a physical cable
B. Through virtual network peering
C. With a network interface card
D. By employing a third-party VPN

383. What is the purpose of subnets within a virtual network?
A. To provide public IP addresses to all Azure resources
B. To increase the cost of the Azure networking services
C. To segment the virtual network into sub-networks and improve address allocation efficiency
D. To replace Network Security Groups

384. What is a VPN gateway in Azure?
A. A gateway that provides a secure connection to the public internet
B. A device that physically connects on-premises networks to Azure
C. A virtual network gateway used to send encrypted traffic between Azure

and an on-premises location over the internet

D. A service that replaces all on-premises networking equipment

385. Can a single virtual network have more than one VPN gateway?

A. Yes, multiple VPN gateways can be created

B. No, only one VPN gateway is allowed per virtual network

C. Yes, but only in different regions

D. No, VPN gateways are not allowed in virtual networks

386. What can you configure in Azure to treat a virtual network like your own network?

A. Virtual machines

B. Physical hardware settings

C. Virtual networks and gateways through software

D. Third-party network services

387. What is the role of a Network Security Group (NSG) in Azure?

A. To allocate IP addresses to Azure resources

B. To manage virtual machine storage

C. To allow or deny inbound network traffic to Azure resources

D. To provide a VPN connection for Azure resources

388. How can Network Security Groups improve the security of your virtual network?

A. By assigning public IP addresses to every resource

B. By accepting traffic only from trusted IP addresses

C. By peering with other virtual networks

D. By encrypting all data in the virtual network

389. Which ports do the VM in the web tier allow inbound traffic on, according to the provided context?

A. Ports 80 (HTTP) and 443 (HTTPS)
B. Ports 22 (SSH) and 80 (HTTP)
C. Ports 25 (SMTP) and 110 (POP3)
D. Ports 53 (DNS) and 143 (IMAP)

390. What can you do with a virtual network in Azure?
A. Only deploy resources in the cloud
B. Connect to other networks in the private IP address space
C. Restrict your network to communication within Azure only
D. Provide unrestricted access to the Internet for all resources

391. What is the primary goal of High Availability (HA) in technology infrastructure?
A. To ensure all software updates are applied immediately
B. To maintain a service up and running for a long period
C. To prevent unauthorized access to systems
D. To perform regular system maintenance

392. What is Fault Tolerance in the context of computer systems?
A. The ability of a system to limit user access during peak traffic
B. The capability of a system to continue operations immediately after a component failure
C. A procedure to update software without service interruption
D. A practice to regularly backup system data

393. What is the main difference between High Availability and Fault Tolerance?
A. High Availability ensures system security, while Fault Tolerance does not
B. Fault Tolerance guarantees the correct end state of an action, while High Availability does not

C. High Availability is easier to implement than Fault Tolerance
D. Fault Tolerance focuses on backup, whereas High Availability focuses on maintenance

394. What is a Load Balancer used for in technology infrastructures?
A. To distribute traffic evenly across a pool of systems
B. To backup data in real-time
C. To detect and prevent cyberattacks
D. To perform automatic software updates

395. What is the purpose of Disaster Recovery (DR)?
A. To provide additional computational resources during peak traffic
B. To ensure continuity and recovery of systems after a disruptive event
C. To guarantee perfect uptime under all conditions
D. To reduce the costs associated with system maintenance

396. How does a Load Balancer contribute to system maintenance?
A. By performing automatic software updates
B. By enabling maintenance tasks without service interruption
C. By storing additional backup data
D. By encrypting data traffic

397. What is Redundancy in the context of Fault Tolerance?
A. The unnecessary repetition of tasks within a system
B. The duplication of critical components or functions of a system
C. The process of compressing data to save storage space
D. The method of spreading traffic across different networks

398. What type of conditions does Resiliency allow a system to withstand?
A. Only natural disasters

B. Only cyberattacks like DDoS.

C. Only system maintenance and software updates

D. A range of abnormal conditions, including natural disasters and cyberattacks

399. Why might a business still require a Disaster Recovery infrastructure even with HA or FT configurations?

A. Because HA and FT cannot protect against cyberattacks

B. Because HA and FT are generally considered outdated technologies

C. Because DR provides a complete recovery plan for catastrophic events beyond the scope of HA and FT

D. Because DR is more cost-effective than HA and FT

400. During a maintenance window, what does a Load Balancer do when it detects an unresponsive VM?

A. It shuts down the VM immediately

B. It redirects traffic to the maintenance team

C. It directs traffic to other VMs in the pool

D. It performs a system reboot on the VM

401. What type of Azure service requires the user to manage patching and securing operating systems and software?

A. Platform as a Service (PaaS)

B. Software as a Service (SaaS)

C. Infrastructure as a Service (IaaS)

D. None of the above

402. What does Azure manage for you in a Platform as a Service (PaaS) offering?

A. Virtual networks only

B. Operating systems and foundational software

C. Security patches for user applications

D. Internet infrastructure

403. What advantage does Platform as a Service (PaaS) provide in terms of operations?

A. It requires manual construction of infrastructures

B. It offers point-and-click solutions within the Azure portal

C. It does not allow for automated scripting

D. It decreases security with automated updates

404. Which Azure service is used by Contoso Shipping for ingesting telemetry data from drones and trucks?

A. Azure Virtual Machines

B. Azure Cosmos DB

C. Azure Event Hubs

D. Microsoft Entra ID

405. What is the primary goal of a defense in-depth strategy?

A. To provide a single layer of robust protection.

B. To slow the advance of an attack and protect data.

C. To eliminate the need for security monitoring.

D. To offer a simple security solution

406. How is the defense-in-depth strategy visualized according to the text?

A. As a linear progression of security measures.

B. As a set of concentric rings.

C. As a complex algorithm.

D. As a single, impenetrable barrier

407. What is the main target for attackers that the defense-in-depth strategy aims to protect?
A. User credentials
B. Network traffic
C. Data
D. Software applications

408. What type of Azure service is demonstrated by an Azure Cosmos DB backend in a web app?
A. Infrastructure as a Service (IaaS)
B. Platform as a Service (PaaS)
C. Software as a Service (SaaS)
D. Database as a Service (DBaaS)

409. Which Azure service level outsources almost all aspects, including the software and internet infrastructure?
A. Infrastructure as a Service (IaaS)
B. Platform as a Service (PaaS)
C. Software as a Service (SaaS)
D. Database as a Service (DBaaS)

410. What is often dictated by regulatory requirements in the context of data security?
A. The location of data centers
B. The types of data that can be stored
C. The controls and processes to ensure data security
D. The pricing of data storage services

411. What is the primary focus of securing the compute layer in application development?
A. Limiting user access to applications
B. Filtering content on websites

C. Securing virtual machine access and implementing endpoint protection

D. Increasing the network bandwidth

412. What is recommended to help reduce lateral movement throughout your network?

A. Increasing the complexity of the network

B. Limiting communication between resources

C. Expanding outbound internet access

D. Removing all firewalls

413. What is a key strategy to protect against network-based attacks at the perimeter layer?

A. Disabling all security firewalls

B. Using distributed denial of service (DDoS) protection

C. Implementing open-source software

D. Encouraging public Internet access

414. In the context of identity and access management, what is a recommended practice?

A. Using the same password across multiple services

B. Disabling multi-factor authentication for convenience

C. Control access to infrastructure and implement change control

D. Limiting audit events and change logs

415. What is the intent of implementing physical security measures?

A. To provide a welcoming atmosphere for visitors

B. To enhance the visual appeal of the data center

C. To offer physical safeguards against access to assets

D. To reduce the cost of digital security measures

416. What is an effective method to keep systems secure from malware?
A. Ignoring software updates
B. Implementing endpoint protection
C. Using simple passwords
D. Granting admin rights to all users

417. What should be restricted to minimize security risks in networking?
A. Inbound internet access
B. Use of secure protocols
C. Regular data backups
D. Internal communication

418. What aspect of security is reinforced by using multi-factor authentication?
A. Network throughput
B. Identity and access security
C. Physical security
D. Web content filtering

419. What is the benefit of implementing DDoS protection at the network perimeter?
A. It increases the speed of the network.
B. It filters large-scale attacks to prevent service denial.
C. It simplifies network configuration.
D. It reduces the need for internal security protocols

420. Why is it important to audit events and changes in the context of identity and access?
A. To track the performance of applications
B. To ensure compliance and security by recording access and changes
C. To provide employees with detailed work logs

D. To advertise the security measures in place

421. What does 'data in transit' refer to?
A. Data stored securely on a physical disk.
B. Data is actively moving between locations, such as across the internet.
C. Data that has been archived for long-term storage.
D. Data being processed by an application in real-time.

422. Which Azure feature automatically encrypts data before it is persisted to storage solutions like Azure Blob storage?
A. Azure Disk Encryption
B. Transparent Data Encryption
C. Azure Storage Service Encryption
D. Azure Key Vault

423. Which feature does Azure Disk Encryption leverage for Windows virtual machine disks?
A. dm-crypt
B. Azure Key Vault
C. BitLocker
D. TDE

424. What is the purpose of Transparent Data Encryption (TDE) in Azure?
A. To manage SSL/TLS certificates
B. To store application secrets in a centralized location
C. To encrypt virtual machine disks in real-time
D. To perform real-time encryption of databases and associated backups

425. By default, how does Azure handle the encryption key for Transparent Data Encryption?
A. It provides a unique encryption key per database
B. It requires users to create their encryption key

C. It provides a unique encryption key per logical SQL Server instance

D. It uses a public encryption key shared across multiple databases

426. What is Azure Key Vault primarily used for?

A. To encrypt data in transit

B. To manage storage account keys exclusively

C. To store and control access to secrets, keys, and certificates

D. To provide real-time encryption for virtual machine disks

427. Which of the following can be stored in Azure Key Vault?

A. Only encryption keys and SSL/TLS certificates

B. Only passwords and connection strings

C. Tokens, passwords, certificates, API keys, and other secrets

D. Virtual machine configurations and network settings

428. What type of security modules does Azure Key Vault allow you to store secrets and keys in?

A. Software-based modules only

B. FIPS 140-2 Level 2 validated HSMs only

C. Both software-based modules and FIPS 140-2 Level 2 validated HSMs

D. TPM (Trusted Platform Module) only

429. What is the benefit of centralizing storage for application secrets in Azure Key Vault?

A. It increases the chances that secrets may be accidentally leaked

B. It decentralizes control over application secrets

C. It reduces the chances that secrets may be accidentally leaked

D. It makes the system less complex and easier to manage

430. How does Azure help provide network security for your environment?

A. By offering Transparent Data Encryption for network traffic

B. By only encrypting data at rest

C. By integrating a layered approach into the network architecture

D. By using Azure Key Vault exclusively for network security

431. What is the primary purpose of Microsoft Defender for Cloud?

A. To provide a messaging system within Azure

B. To manage virtual machine storage

C. To identify internet-facing resources that are not secure

D. To automate software deployment

432. Which Azure service is a fully stateful firewall as a service?

A. Azure Application Gateway

B. Azure DDoS Protection

C. Microsoft Defender for Cloud

D. Azure Firewall

433. What type of protection does Azure Application Gateway offer?

A. Inbound and outbound network-level protection

B. Protection from DDoS attacks

C. Protection from common exploits and vulnerabilities in websites

D. Protection for non-HTTP/S protocols

434. What is not recommended when deploying Azure Firewall in terms of global VNet peering?

A. Deploying one firewall per region

B. Using a hub-and-spoke model

C. Peering across regions

D. Centralizing control across different subscriptions

435. What are the three types of rule collections available in Azure Firewall?

A. Application rules, Protocol rules, and Service rules

B. Intrusion rules, NAT rules, and Network rules

C. NAT rules, Network rules, and Application rules

D. Filtering rules, Routing rules, and Connection rules

436. What is Azure DDoS Protection designed to defend against?

A. SQL injection attacks

B. Unauthorized data access

C. Malware infections

D. Denial of service attacks

437. What type of attack does the DDoS Protection Standard mitigate by absorbing and scrubbing with Azure's global network scale?

A. Resource (application) layer attacks

B. Volumetric attacks

C. Protocol attacks

D. Insider threats

438. Which type of Azure Firewall rules are applied first when network traffic enters the firewall?

A. Application rules

B. Network rules

C. NAT rules

D. Security rules

439. What is the main difference between Network Security Groups (NSGs) and Azure Firewalls?

A. NSGs provide application-level protection, while Azure Firewall provides network-level protection

B. NSGs provide centralized network firewall capabilities, while Azure

Firewall provides distributed network layer filtering

C. NSGs provide distributed network layer traffic filtering within virtual networks, while Azure Firewall offers centralized, stateful firewall capabilities

D. NSGs are for outbound protection only, whereas Azure Firewall is for both inbound and outbound protection

440. In the context of DDoS Protection, which type of attack targets the web application packets to disrupt data transmission between hosts?
A. Volumetric attacks
B. Protocol attacks
C. Resource (application) layer attacks
D. NAT rule exploitation

441. What is the primary purpose of Network Security Groups (NSGs) within an Azure virtual network?
A. To manage virtual machine sizes
B. To restrict communication between resources
C. To allocate more bandwidth to certain resources
D. To assign public IP addresses to virtual machines

442. How can Azure service access be limited to your virtual network?
A. By using Microsoft Entra ID
B. Through the application of Azure Labels
C. By restricting access to service endpoints
D. By configuring Azure Advanced Threat Protection

443. What is Azure ExpressRoute primarily used for?
A. To create a public internet access point
B. To extend on-premises networks into the Microsoft cloud over a private connection

C. For dynamic routing between virtual networks

D. As an alternative to Azure Advanced Threat Protection

444. What can Azure Information Protection (AIP) do with classified content?

A. Increase bandwidth for content transfer

B. Assign public IP addresses to content

C. Track and control how content is used

D. Automatically delete content after a certain period

445. Which technology is used by Azure Information Protection to apply protection to documents and emails?

A. Azure Advanced Threat Protection

B. Microsoft Entra ID

C. Azure Rights Management (Azure RMS)

D. Network Security Groups (NSGs)

446. What type of connections does Azure ExpressRoute facilitate?

A. Public internet connections

B. Wireless mobile connections

C. Private connections with a connectivity provider

D. Satellite communication links

447. How does Azure Advanced Threat Protection help security professionals?

A. By providing a dedicated VPN connection

B. By managing network traffic through NSGs

C. By identifying, detecting, and investigating advanced threats and compromised identities

D. By encrypting files using Azure Rights Management

448. What can be controlled using the labels applied by Microsoft Azure Information Protection?
A. The size of the documents and emails
B. The geographical location of the data storage
C. The bandwidth usage of the network
D. The access and usage of documents and emails

449. What does Azure ExpressRoute improve by using a private connection?
A. The speed of Azure Advanced Threat Protection
B. The security of on-premises communication to Microsoft cloud services
C. The encryption level of Azure Information Protection
D. The traffic handling capacity of Network Security Groups

450. What does Azure Advanced Threat Protection monitor to help detect advanced attacks?
A. The allocation of NSGs in the network
B. The physical hardware changes in the network
C. User, entity behavior and activities with learning-based analytics
D. The uptime and downtime of virtual machines

451. What is the purpose of a policy assignment in Azure?
A. To define a new policy
B. To charge for the Azure services
C. To assign a policy definition within a specific scope
D. To create a new Azure resource

452. What happens when a policy is applied to a resource group?
A. It charges the resource group
B. It is only applied to the resource group, not the resources within it

C. It is inherited by all child resources within that resource group

D. It is ignored by all child resources within that resource group

453. Can you exclude a sub-scope from a policy assignment in Azure?

A. No, exclusions are not -possible.

B. Yes, but only at the subscription level.

C. Yes, but only for resource groups.

D. Yes, you can exclude a sub-scope from the policy assignment.

454. Which Azure tool can you use to assign policies?

A. Azure Monitor

B. Azure Portal, PowerShell, or Azure CLI

C. Visual Studio

D. Azure Storage Explorer

455. What effect does the 'Deny' policy effect have in Azure Policy?

A. It appends additional fields to resources

B. It audits the resource creation/update process

C. It prevents resource creation/update if it violates the policy

D. It triggers a deployment if a certain condition is not met

456. What is the result of the 'Audit' policy effect in Azure?

A. It results in an automatic fix of the non-compliance

B. It creates a warning event in the activity log

C. It prevents the creation of non-compliant resources

D. It charges the user for non-compliance

457. What is an initiative definition in Azure Policy?

A. A single policy definition with a wide scope

B. A financial plan for Azure resources

C. A group of policy definitions to help track compliance for a larger goal

D. A template deployment that is executed when a condition is met

458. What is the recommended use of initiatives in Azure Policy?

A. Only when you have a single policy definition

B. When you need to charge for policy usage

C. When you have more than a few policy definitions or expect to increase the number over time

D. When you want to disable all policy effects

459. Where in the Azure portal can you find the Azure Policy section?

A. In the "Monitoring" section

B. In the "Authoring" section

C. Through the search field or under All Services

D. In the "Deployment" section

460. What does the 'DeployIfNotExists' policy effect do?

A. It audits a resource if it doesn't exist

B. It charges for the resources that don't exist

C. It creates a resource if it doesn't exist

D. It executes a template deployment when a specific condition is met

461. What is the primary benefit of using Azure Blueprints over Azure Resource Manager Templates?

A. Azure Blueprints are easier to set up

B. Azure Blueprints maintain an active relationship with deployed resources

C. Azure Blueprints are the only way to deploy resources

D. Azure Resource Manager Templates do not support role assignments

462. What can Azure Blueprints help you with in terms of deployments?
A. Reducing costs of resources
B. Increasing the speed of development
C. Eliminating the need for policies
D. Avoiding any compliance requirements

463. What artifacts can you include in an Azure Blueprint?
A. Virtual Machines only
B. Databases and Containers
C. Resource groups, Role assignments, Policy assignments, Azure Resource Manager templates
D. Only Azure Resource Manager templates

464. How are Azure Blueprints different from Azure Resource Manager Templates in terms of storage and deployment?
A. Blueprints can only be stored locally
B. Resource Manager Templates cannot be stored in source control
C. Resource Manager Templates have no active connection to deployed resources
D. Blueprints cannot be versioned or composed through a CI/CD pipeline

465. What is the purpose of role assignments in Azure Blueprints?
A. To automatically delete users from groups
B. To assign a policy or initiative to the blueprint
C. To ensure that the right people always have the right access to resources
D. To create new virtual machines

466. Can Azure Blueprints upgrade multiple subscriptions at once?
A. Yes, if the same blueprint governs them
B. No, each subscription must be upgraded individually
C. Azure Blueprints do not support upgrades

D. Only if the subscriptions are in the same resource group

467. What is the purpose of the Microsoft Trust Center?
A. To process personal data
B. To sell Microsoft products
C. To provide full transparency on how Microsoft manages underlying resources
D. To offer discounts on services

468. Which of the following is NOT a supported artifact type in Azure Blueprint?
A. Virtual Networks
B. Resource Groups
C. Policy Assignments
D. Role Assignments

469. What is the function of the Microsoft Privacy Statement?
A. To define the costs of Microsoft services
B. To explain what personal data Microsoft processes and for what purposes
C. To provide a list of all Microsoft products and services
D. To describe Microsoft's organizational structure

470. What is the relationship between a blueprint definition and a blueprint assignment in Azure Blueprints?
A. They refer to the same thing and are interchangeable
B. The definition specifies what should be deployed; the assignment shows what was deployed
C. The assignment is the initial setup, while the definition is the final deployment
D. The definition is used for billing purposes, while the assignment is for resource allocation

471. What is the primary purpose of Azure Monitor?
A. To automate the deployment of applications
B. To collect and analyze telemetry from cloud and on-premises environments
C. To provide cloud storage solutions
D. To manage Azure subscription billing

472. Which types of data does Azure Monitor collect?
A. Only application monitoring data
B. Only guest OS monitoring data
C. Metrics and logs from various tiers, including application and OS
D. Only Azure subscription monitoring data

473. What are metrics in the context of Azure Monitor?
A. Records with a set of properties for analysis
B. Numerical values that describe a system at a particular time
C. Data storage systems for large amounts of information
D. Automated responses to system events

474. Which service is designed to monitor the performance of container workloads in Azure Kubernetes Service (AKS)?
A. Azure Monitor for VMs
B. Application Insights
C. Azure Monitor for containers
D. Azure Service Health

475. What does Application Insights provide?
A. Management of Azure subscription billing
B. Monitoring of Azure storage accounts

C. Insights into web applications' availability, performance, and usage

D. Real-time data storage solutions

476. How can Azure Monitor proactively notify you of critical conditions?

A. Through Azure Service Health

B. By deploying new resources

C. Using alerts and Auto-scale

D. By applying updates to applications

477. What is Azure Status?

A. A tool to monitor the performance of VMs

B. A global view of the health state of Azure services

C. A dashboard for resource deployment

D. A security feature for Azure applications

478. What kind of insights does Azure Service Health provide?

A. Insights on the most profitable Azure services

B. Personalized guidance and support when Azure service issues affect users

C. Analysis of user behavior within Azure applications

D. Data on the geographic distribution of Azure data centers

479. What is the purpose of Resource Health in Azure Service Health?

A. To provide global updates on all Azure resources

B. To manage Azure service billing and subscriptions

C. To diagnose and support when Azure service issues affect resources

D. To monitor the physical health of data center resources

480. What is the benefit of integrating monitoring services with Azure Service Health?

A. It provides faster data storage options

B. It ensures compliance with data protection laws

C. It offers insights into the health status of Azure services impacting your environment

D. It allows unlimited data transfer between different Azure services

481. What is the primary function of tags in managing Azure resources?
A. To encrypt data
B. To schedule automated jobs
C. To organize resources for billing or management
D. To increase the speed of virtual machines

482. How can tags be useful in a monitoring system?
A. By increasing the frequency of alerts
B. By including tag data with alerts to identify impacted resources
C. By preventing alerts from being triggered
D. By automatically resolving alerts without human intervention

483. What can Azure Policy enforce regarding resource creation?
A. The physical location of the data center
B. The content within the virtual machines
C. The types of resources that can be created
D. The color scheme of the Azure portal

484. What is a use case for tags in Azure Automation?
A. To encrypt virtual machines
B. To color-code resources
C. To automate the shutdown and startup of virtual machines
D. To track the number of users accessing a resource

485. How does IT governance relate to Azure Policy?
A. It provides decorative themes for Azure resources
B. It offers a gaming platform for Azure users
C. It ensures effective and efficient use of IT to achieve organizational goals
D. It manages social media accounts for Azure resources

486. What can Azure Policy restrict in terms of geographic deployment?
A. The weather conditions for deployment
B. The Azure regions where resources can be deployed
C. The language settings for deployed resources
D. The time zone settings for virtual machines

487. How can Azure Policy help with cost management in development environments?
A. By enforcing the use of premium storage accounts
B. By restricting the deployment of large VM sizes
C. By providing unlimited budgets for resource creation
D. By mandating the use of the most expensive resources

488. What is the consequence of NOT using standardized naming conventions in Azure?
A. Increased security risks
B. Inability to use Azure services
C. Inconsistent naming across resources
D. Automatic deletion of unnamed resources

489. What is the advantage of including specific tags on resources when exporting billing data?
A. Tags exclude resources from the billing report
B. Tags provide detailed network configurations
C. Tags allow for more granular analysis of costs
D. Tags automatically pay the billing invoices

490. What role do tags play in the automation of virtual machines in Azure?
A. They act as a firewall for virtual machines
B. They determine the operating system of virtual machines
C. They assist in automating operational tasks like shutdown and startup
D. They increase the computational power of virtual machines

491. What is the first step when using the TCO calculator for Azure?
A. Adjust assumptions
B. View the report
C. Define your workloads
D. Save on infrastructure costs

492. What type of details should you enter for the 'Servers' group in the TCO calculator?
A. Details of your Azure server infrastructure
B. Details of your on-premises storage infrastructure
C. Details of your on-premises server infrastructure
D. Amount of network bandwidth consumption

493. Which Azure service should you select in the 'Destination' section for databases in the TCO calculator?
A. The corresponding on-premises service
B. Any Azure service based on preference
C. The corresponding Azure service you would like to use
D. The most cost-effective Azure service

494. Which cost assumptions can be adjusted in the TCO calculator to improve accuracy?
A. Virtualization costs

B. Storage and IT labor costs

C. Database and networking costs

D. Data center costs

495. What does the TCO calculator report allow you to compare?

A. Different Azure services

B. The costs of different Visual Studio subscriptions

C. On-premises infrastructure costs with Azure cloud costs

D. The efficiency of on-premises infrastructure with Azure

496. What is the benefit of activating Azure credits for Visual Studio subscribers?

A. It reduces the cost of on-premises infrastructure.

B. It allows for unlimited usage of Azure services.

C. It provides a monthly credit for testing new solutions on Azure.

D. It offers a permanent discount on Azure services

497. How does the monthly Azure credit benefit work for Visual Studio subscribers?

A. It provides a one-time credit upon subscription.

B. It offers a discount on Azure services based on usage.

C. It allows for a fixed discount on all Azure services.

D. It renews a monthly credit balance each month while active

498. What type of Azure services can be tried out with the Azure credits from a Visual Studio subscription?

A. Only Visual Studio IDE and related services

B. Only basic services such as computing and storage

C. A variety of services, including App Service and Azure SQL Server databases

D. Exclusively networking and security services

499. What is the purpose of adjusting assumptions in the TCO calculator?
A. To get a general idea of Azure services
B. To customize the report based on user preference
C. To improve the accuracy of the TCO calculator
D. To reduce the number of services in the report

500. What action is recommended after creating cost estimates and analyzing current expenses in Azure?
A. Ignoring the projected future expenses
B. Increasing the budget for Azure services
C. Looking at how to reduce infrastructure costs
D. Switching back to on-premises solutions

VERSAtile Reads

Answers

1. Answer: B

Explanation: Cloud computing primarily allows users to rent computing resources, such as storage and CPU cycles, rather than having to purchase and maintain physical hardware. Users pay only for what they use.

2. Answer: B

Explanation: A virtual machine is an emulation of a computer system that includes its operating system and hardware, which appears to the user like a physical computer.

3. Answer: C

Explanation: The difference between a VM and a physical computer is that the VM is hosted on a cloud provider's server, and users do not need to buy any hardware or install the OS themselves.

4. Answer: C

Explanation: In cloud computing, containers are packages that include an application and all its dependencies, but unlike VMs, they don't require a guest operating system, instead using a standard runtime environment.

5. Answer: B

Explanation: Serverless computing is a cloud computing execution model where the cloud provider runs the server and dynamically manages the allocation of machine resources, allowing users to run application code without maintaining a server.

6. Answer: C

Explanation: Serverless computing is ideal for automated tasks because it allows for applications to be broken down into separate functions that run when triggered, which is perfect for tasks like automatically sending emails after an online purchase.

7. Answer: B

Explanation: VMs and containers are charged while they're running, regardless of whether the applications on them are active or idle, which differs from the serverless model.

8. Answer: B

Explanation: The main advantage of using a VM in the cloud is the quick setup time and the cost-efficiency compared to purchasing and setting up a physical computer.

9. Answer: D

Explanation: Serverless computing charges users only for the processing time each function uses as it executes, which is a different pricing model compared to VMs and containers.

10. Answer: D

Explanation: While distributed databases are a component of cloud services, they are not a computing choice like VMs, containers, or serverless computing. They are more related to data storage and management.

11. **Answer: B**

Explanation: The text describes a consumption-based pricing model where you only pay for the resources that you actually use, which is synonymous with the pay-as-you-go pricing model.

12. **Answer: C**

Explanation: 'Scaling up' or vertical scaling refers to the process of adding more resources, such as CPUs or memory, to increase the power of an existing server.

13. **Answer: C**

Explanation: Elasticity in cloud computing allows for automatically adding or removing resources as the workload changes, which can happen due to a spike or drop in demand

14. **Answer: C**

Explanation: Cloud computing is considered 'current' because it removes the need to maintain software patches, hardware setup, upgrades, and other time-consuming IT management chores.

15. **Answer: B**

Explanation: Cloud computing providers ensure data reliability by offering services like data backup, disaster recovery, and data replication to protect data at all times.

16. Answer: C

Explanation: Redundancy built into cloud services architecture enhances fault tolerance by ensuring that a backup component takes over if one component fails, preventing impact on customers.

17. Answer: C

Explanation: Cloud providers have fully redundant data centers located in multiple regions worldwide, enabling services to have a local presence near customers and the best response times.

18. Answer: C

Explanation: Horizontal scaling, or 'scaling out,' is the process of adding more servers that work together as one unit, such as when handling incoming requests.

19. Answer: C

Explanation: Cloud providers offer a broad set of policies, technologies, controls, and expertise that can provide better security than what most organizations can achieve on their own.

20. Answer: B

Explanation: Resource scaling can be done automatically in cloud computing, where resources are allocated or de-allocated based on specific triggers such as CPU utilization or the number of requests.

21. Answer: A

Explanation: Capital Expenditure (CapEx) refers to the spending of money on the physical infrastructure upfront, with the expense being deducted from the tax bill over time. It is an initial investment that decreases in value over time.

22. Answer: C

Explanation: Operational Expenditure (OpEx) involves spending money on services or products and being billed for them now, allowing the expense to be deducted from the tax bill in the same year. There are no upfront costs, and payment is made as services or products are used.

23. Answer: C

Explanation: The benefit of Capital Expenditure (CapEx) is that expenses are planned at the start of a project, allowing for fixed costs and precise budgeting before a project begins.

24. Answer: C

Explanation: Operational Expenditure (OpEx) is more appealing when the demand for services or products fluctuates or is unknown because costs are managed dynamically and can adjust to changing needs without large upfront investments.

25. Answer: B

Explanation: In cloud computing, Operational Expenditure (OpEx) typically includes leasing cloud-based servers and software features, along with other usage-based services such as backup and archive, disaster recovery, and employing technical personnel on a non-permanent basis.

26. Answer: B

Explanation: Leasing a data center infrastructure is generally associated with Capital Expenditure (CapEx) because it involves an upfront investment in physical assets. However, in some contexts, it could be considered an operational cost depending on the specific financial arrangement.

27. Answer: B

Explanation: Operational Expenditure (OpEx) is characterized by having no upfront cost. Payments for services or products occur as they are used, and the expense can be deducted in the same year it is incurred.

28. Answer: B

Explanation: Economies of scale in cloud computing mean that the cost per unit decreases as the scale of operation increases, allowing for a more cost-effective operations at larger scales.

29. Answer: C

Explanation: Capital Expenditure (CapEx) involves deducting the expense over time as the value of the upfront investment in physical infrastructure reduces. Operational Expenditure (OpEx) allows for an immediate deduction from the tax bill in the same year the expense is incurred.

30. **Answer: D**

Explanation: A business might choose Capital Expenditure (CapEx) over Operational Expenditure (OpEx) when it needs to predict expenses and budget accurately before a project starts, as CapEx involves planned expenses and fixed costs.

31. **Answer: B**

Explanation: The public cloud offers high scalability and agility, which means that resources can be easily scaled up or down based on demand, and new services or applications can be quickly deployed. There is no need to manage physical hardware, as everything runs on the cloud provider's infrastructure.

32. **Answer: C**

Explanation: The public cloud may not meet certain security requirements. Some organizations have specific security needs that cannot be satisfied by public cloud offerings due to government policies, industry standards, or legal requirements.

33. **Answer: C**

Explanation: Private clouds are often used when organizations need to meet strict security, compliance, or legal requirements because they want to have full control over their environment, including the data center, hardware, and software services.

34. **Answer: C**

Answers

VERSAtile Reads

Explanation: The private cloud requires some initial capital expenditure (CapEx) costs to purchase the necessary hardware and software for startup and ongoing maintenance, unlike the public cloud, which generally operates on a pay-as-you-go pricing model.

35. Answer: C

Explanation: Hybrid cloud deployments allow organizations to maintain systems that may be running on outdated hardware or operating systems by combining resources from both public and private clouds.

36. Answer: B

Explanation: Hybrid cloud models allow organizations to take advantage of the economies of scale offered by public cloud providers, which can often result in cost savings for services and resources. For some workloads, it's cheaper to use public cloud resources supplemented by private infrastructure when necessary.

37. Answer: C

Explanation: The private cloud model provides organizations with maximum control over their environment because they own and manage the data center, hardware, and software services, which enables them to ensure that the configuration can support any specific scenario or legacy application.

38. Answer: C

Explanation: Hybrid clouds can be more complicated to set up and manage due to their nature of combining public and private cloud resources. This complexity requires careful planning and potentially more sophisticated IT skills and expertise.

39. **Answer: B**

Explanation: In a private cloud, agility is limited because scaling up requires purchasing, installing, and setting up new hardware, which takes more time compared to the public cloud, where resources can be scaled up or down quickly through the service provider

40. **Answer: C**

Explanation: An organization might opt for a hybrid cloud deployment to fulfill particular business requirements, such as meeting specific security, compliance, or legacy application needs, where they need to completely control the environment using their equipment while still benefiting from the public cloud for other less sensitive tasks

41. **Answer: C**

Explanation: IaaS is the most flexible cloud service category aimed at giving users complete control over the hardware that runs their applications. It allows users to rent hardware rather than purchasing it outright, providing an instant computing infrastructure that is provisioned and managed over the internet.

42. **Answer: C**

Explanation: PaaS provides an environment for building, testing, and deploying software applications where the cloud provider manages the server and infrastructure, allowing users to focus on the development of their applications without worrying about the underlying systems.

43. **Answer. C**

Explanation: SaaS is typically licensed through a subscription model where users pay on a monthly or annual basis. This model allows users to use the application software without being responsible for its maintenance or management.

44. **Answer: B**

Explanation: In a PaaS offering, the cloud provider is responsible for operating system management, network, and service configuration. This allows the user to concentrate on developing their applications rather than managing the infrastructure.

45. **Answer: C**

Explanation: In an IaaS model, the user is responsible for managing the operating systems, data, and applications. The cloud provider, on the other hand, ensures that the underlying cloud infrastructure is available for the user.

46. **Answer: C**

Explanation: SaaS requires the least amount of management from the user. The cloud provider is responsible for managing everything, including provision, management, and maintenance of the application software, while the user uses the software.

47. **Answer: C**

Explanation: The main advantage of using PaaS over IaaS is that it requires less user management. With PaaS, the cloud provider manages the operating systems, allowing the user to focus on developing their applications.

48. Answer: C

Explanation: With IaaS, there are no upfront costs. Users pay only for what they consume, which refers to the infrastructure resources they use, such as computing power, storage, and networking.

49. Answer: C

Explanation: A SaaS user is only responsible for using the application software. The cloud provider takes care of the provision, management, and maintenance of the application software.

50. Answer: D

Explanation: IaaS serves as the foundational layer upon which PaaS is built. PaaS uses the infrastructure provided by IaaS and adds additional layers such as development frameworks, middleware, and other tools that facilitate application development and deployment.

51. Answer: C

Explanation: Azure Kubernetes Service (AKS) is designed for the management of a cluster of VMs that run containerized services, allowing for scalable and efficient deployment and management of containerized applications

52. Answer: B

Explanation: Azure Load Balancer is specifically designed to balance inbound and outbound connections to applications or service endpoints, ensuring high availability and reliability.

53. Answer: C

Explanation: Azure Blob Storage is ideal for storing very large objects, such as video files or bitmaps, offering scalable, durable, and highly available storage solutions.

54. Answer: A

Explanation: Azure SQL Database is a fully managed relational database service that comes with auto-scaling capabilities, integral intelligence, and robust security, making it a sophisticated solution for database management in the cloud.

55. Answer: B

Explanation: Azure IoT Hub is a messaging hub that enables secure and reliable communication and monitoring between millions of IoT devices and the cloud.

56. Answer: B

Explanation: Azure Machine Learning Studio offers a collaborative, drag-and-drop visual workspace to build, test, and deploy machine learning solutions with ease, without the need for extensive coding.

57. Answer: C

Explanation: Azure Content Delivery Network is designed to deliver high-bandwidth content to users around the world, reducing latency and improving user experience.

58. Answer: C

Explanation: Azure ExpressRoute facilitates a dedicated and private connection to Azure, bypassing the public internet for more reliable and secure connectivity.

59. Answer: C

Explanation: Azure SQL Data Warehouse is tailored for running analytics on a large scale, utilizing massive parallel processing to quickly run complex queries across petabytes of data.

60. Answer: A

Explanation: Azure SignalR Service is a specific service designed to help developers add real-time web functionalities, such as live chat and real-time dashboard updates, to their applications with ease.

61. Answer: B

Explanation: Azure Cloud Shell is described as a browser-based command-line tool that allows users to manage and develop Azure resources interactively in the cloud.

62. Answer: C

Explanation: Cloud Shell provides two types of command-line experiences: Bash and PowerShell, both of which come with access to the Azure CLI.

63. Answer: A

Explanation: The command 'az group create' along with parameters like `--name` and `--location` is used to create a new resource group in Azure.

64. Answer: C

Explanation: The command specifies the image as Win2019Datacenter, which is a Windows Server 2019 image, and the size as Standard_DS2_v2, which has two virtual CPUs and 7 GB of memory.

65. Answer: C

Explanation: To verify that a VM is running, you can use the 'az vm get-instance-view' command with the appropriate VM name and resource group, which will display the VM's provisioning and power state.

66. Answer: B

Explanation: The 'az vm create' command includes the creation and assignment of a public IP address to the VM by default unless specifically configured not to do so.

67. Answer: C

Explanation: Regions in Azure refer to a set of data centers located in a specific geographic area. Every Azure resource is assigned a region.

68. **Answer: B**

Explanation: The size of a VM in Azure defines its technical specifications, such as processor speed, memory, storage capacity, and expected network bandwidth.

69. **Answer: B**

Explanation: Resource groups in Azure are logical containers used to organize related resources, such as VMs, disks, and network interfaces that make up an application or service. They enable easier administration and management as a unit.

70. **Answer: B**

Explanation: IIS is a web server that runs on Windows and is used to serve standard web content such as HTML, CSS, and JavaScript, as well as to run ASP.NET and other web applications.

71. **Answer: B**

Explanation: The Custom Script Extension for Azure VMs allows you to download and run scripts to automate deployments, which can be stored in Azure storage or a public location such as GitHub.

72. **Answer: C**

Explanation: The command `az vm extension set` is used along with additional parameters to download and execute a PowerShell script on an Azure VM using the Custom Script Extension.

73. **Answer: C**

Explanation: The command `dism /online /enable-feature /featurename: IIS-WebServerRole` is used in a PowerShell script to install IIS on a Windows Server.

74. Answer: A

Explanation: The command `az vm open-port --port 80` is used to open port 80 (HTTP) through the firewall for an Azure VM.

75. Answer: C

Explanation: The command `az vm show --query [publicIps]` is used to list the public IP address of an Azure VM.

76. Answer: C

Explanation: The script sets the content of the home page to a basic HTML page with a welcome message along with the VM's computer name, "myVM".

77. Answer: C

Explanation: The `--settings` parameter is used to specify the location of the scripts that the Custom Script Extension will download and run, such as a URL to a script stored on GitHub.

78. Answer: B

Explanation: The `--protected-settings` parameter is used to specify the command that should be executed by the Custom Script Extension, including setting the execution policy and the script to run.

79. Answer: B

Explanation: After installing IIS with the script and opening port 80, the VM will serve the custom-configured home page over HTTP on port 80.

80. Answer: C

Explanation: The command 'az vm resize' is used to change the size of an existing VM in Azure. The command requires specifying the resource group, VM name, and the new size to which the VM needs to be resized.

81. Answer: D

Explanation: Azure VPN Gateway is a service that enables you to create and manage secure site-to-site connections between on-premises networks and Azure virtual networks. It uses VPN tunnels to ensure secure communication.

82. Answer: C

Explanation: The command 'az vm show' retrieves information about the VM, and when used with the specific query flag as provided, it will show the hardware profile, which includes the size of the VM.

83. Answer: C

Explanation: The '--output tsv' flag indicates that the output format for the command should be Tab-Separated Values (TSV).

84. Answer: B

Answers

Explanation: The '--resource-group' flag is used with Azure CLI commands to specify the resource group under which the VM is located.

85. Answer: A

Explanation: The 'hardware profile' query in the 'az vm show' command refers to the CPU and memory allocation of the VM, which is indicative of the VM size.

86. Answer: B

Explanation: The '--name' flag is used in conjunction with the 'az vm resize' command to specify the name of the virtual machine that you want to resize.

87. Answer: B

Explanation: Azure Role-Based Access Control (RBAC) allows you to manage access to Azure resources by assigning roles to users, groups, and applications. It ensures that only authorized users can access specific resources.

88. Answer: C

Explanation: The '--query "hardware profile"' part of the command is used to filter the output so that it only shows the hardware profile of the VM, which includes information about its size.

89. Answer: C

Explanation: To resize multiple VMs, the VM name in the command must be changed for each VM using the '--name' flag. The resource group could be the same if all VMs are in the same group, and the VM size would remain 'Standard_DS3_v2' if all VMs need to be resized to that size. The query remains the same, as it is only used to verify the size after the resize operation.

90. Answer: B

Explanation: Getting involved with private or public previews is beneficial as it can help drive products in a direction that is useful for your organization by providing valuable feedback during the product's development stage.

91. Answer: C

Explanation: An Azure region is defined as a geographical area on the planet that contains multiple data centers that are networked together with a low-latency network. This organization allows for better scalability, redundancy, and data residency for services.

92. Answer: C

Explanation: Azure's extensive network of global regions allows users to deploy their applications in locations closer to where their users are, providing lower latency and a better user experience while also offering improved scalability and redundancy.

93. Answer: C

Explanation: Azure geography refers to a discrete market that is typically made up of two or more regions, which are defined by geopolitical boundaries or country borders. This helps in preserving data residency and compliance within those geographical limits.

94. Answer: B

Explanation: Azure geographies are important because they allow customers to meet specific data residency and compliance needs by keeping their data and applications close. They ensure that data residency, sovereignty, compliance, and resiliency requirements are respected within the geographical boundaries.

95. Answer: C

Explanation: Data residency refers to the physical or geographic location where an organization's data is stored. This concept is crucial for complying with legal or regulatory requirements that are imposed on data based on the country or region in which it resides.

96. Answer: B

Explanation: Azure geographies are designed to be fault-tolerant and can withstand complete region failure through their connection to dedicated high-capacity networking infrastructure. This ensures continuous service and compliance with data residency requirements even in the face of regional outages.

97. Answer: C

Explanation: Azure divides the world into geographies that include the Americas, Europe, Asia Pacific, Middle East, and Africa. Each region within these geographies has specific service availability, compliance, and data residency/sovereignty rules applied to it.

Answers

98. Answer: C

Explanation: Organizing data centers into regions allows Azure to intelligently assign and control resources within each region, ensuring that workloads are appropriately balanced. This structure also supports better scalability and redundancy for the services offered.

99. Answer: D

Explanation: Azure regions are geographical areas that can contain multiple data centers networked together with a low-latency network. This interconnected setup helps provide better service and redundancy for deployed applications.

100. Answer: D

Explanation: Although Availability Zones are a part of Azure's infrastructure, providing high availability within regions, they are not explicitly described in the provided context. The context focuses on regions and geographies without detailing Availability Zones.

101. Answer: B

Explanation: Availability Zones in Azure are designed to ensure that services and data remain available and redundant in the case of failures by having physically separate data centers within an Azure region. This allows for continued operation even if one zone goes down.

102. Answer: C

Explanation: Each Availability Zone is made up of one or more data centers that are equipped with independent power, cooling, and networking to ensure isolation and continuous service even if one zone is compromised.

103. Answer: C

Explanation: Availability Zones are connected through high-speed, private fiber-optic networks, enabling fast and secure communication and data transfer between the zones.

104. Answer: B

Explanation: An Availability Set in Azure offers a 99.95% SLA, ensuring that at least one of the virtual machines will be available in case of infrastructure failures

105. Answer: C

Explanation: Availability Zones offer a higher SLA of 99.99%, indicating a higher level of availability compared to Availability Sets due to the virtual machines being located in different physical locations within an Azure Region.

106. Answer: C

Explanation: There is a minimum of three Availability Zones within a single Azure region, each consisting of one or more data centers.

107. Answer: C

Explanation: An Availability Set ensures the availability of virtual machines within the same data center, whereas an Availability Zone provides a higher level of availability because the virtual machines are spread across different physical locations within an Azure Region.

108. **Answers: C**

Explanation: Azure region pairs are designed to replicate resources across geographically separated regions to reduce the chance of service interruptions due to large-scale disasters that could affect both regions at once.

109. **Answer: C**

Explanation: Each Azure region is paired with another region within the same geography, and they are located at least 300 miles apart to ensure geographical isolation from disasters.

110. **Answer: B**

Explanation: Azure Monitor is a service that provides comprehensive monitoring and analytics for applications and services in Azure. It helps you understand the performance and health of your resources and diagnose issues.

111. **Answer: B**

Explanation: SLAs define the specific performance standards that apply to Azure, demonstrating Microsoft's commitment to delivering high-quality products and services with defined performance targets.

112. Answer: C

Explanation: If an Azure service fails to perform to its governing SLA's specification, the SLA outlines that service credits are to be issued to the customer.

113. Answer: D

Explanation: Free upgrade to premium services is not a characteristic of SLAs for Azure. The key characteristics include Performance Targets, Uptime and Connectivity Guarantees, and Service Credits.

114. Answer: D

Explanation: The typical SLA specifies performance target commitments that range from 99.9 percent to 99.999 percent uptime for each corresponding Azure product or service.

115. Answer: C

Explanation: SLAs for individual Azure products and services describe Microsoft's commitment to providing Azure customers with specific performance standards.

116. Answer: B

Explanation: Performance targets for some Azure services are expressed as uptime guarantees or connectivity rates.

117. Answer: C

Explanation: Yes, it is possible to test the next version of the Azure portal as it is made available for public preview, allowing users to provide feedback before it becomes generally available.

118. **Answer: B**

Explanation: SLAs are specific to each Azure product and service, meaning they are not standardized across all products.

119. **Answer: C**

Explanation: An SLA might promise that a service will be available for a certain percentage of time (uptime) and that the service provider will respond to requests within specific time frames (response times). These metrics ensure reliability and accountability.

120. **Answer: B**

Explanation: A performance target of 99.9% uptime is referred to as "three nines" in SLA terminology.

121. **Answer: B**

Explanation: A Composite SLA is the resultant SLA when combining SLAs across different Azure service offerings. It reflects the overall uptime or reliability of an application that relies on multiple Azure services, which can result in higher or lower uptime values depending on the application architecture.

122. **Answer: C**

Explanation: When you combine the SLAs of two services, in this case, 99.95% and 99.99999%, the composite SLA is approximately 99.95%. This example demonstrates that adding a service with a high SLA can improve the overall composite SLA of the application.

123. Answer: B

Explanation: If an Azure product or service underperforms and fails to meet its specified SLA, customers may be compensated with a discount applied to their Azure bill.

124. Answer: C

Explanation: Application reliability can be improved by designing the application in such a way that it can handle failures of dependent services. Creating independent fallback paths, such as queuing transactions when a database is unavailable, can help maintain application availability despite service disruptions.

125. Answer: C

Explanation: Application customers create SLAs to set performance targets that are tailored to the specific needs of their Azure application. It takes into account the performance of various Azure products and services within the solution to create achievable expectations.

126. Answer: B

Explanation: Resiliency is about a system's capacity to handle failures and recover from them to continue functioning. It is not about completely avoiding failures but how the system responds to them to avoid downtime or data loss.

127. Answer: C

Explanation: High availability and disaster recovery are key aspects of a resilient system. High availability ensures that the application remains operational despite issues, while disaster recovery prepares the system to recover from major incidents.

128. Answer: D

Explanation: There is no guarantee that a preview feature will go into General Availability. Features during the preview phase are still being evaluated and may not become fully available products.

129. Answer: C

Explanation: When improving a composite SLA by adding fallback mechanisms such as a queue, the system becomes more resilient to failures and can maintain higher availability. However, this enhancement introduces additional components and logic to the application, increasing its overall complexity. Managing and maintaining these additional components can lead to higher development and operational costs. Thus, while fallback mechanisms improve reliability, they come with the trade-off of making the system more complex and expensive to manage.

130. Answer: B

Explanation: Understanding the Azure SLAs for each product and service used in your solution is essential for setting realistic and achievable performance targets for your Application SLAs. It ensures that the targets you set are in line with the performance guarantees provided by Microsoft for their services.

131. Answer: B

Explanation: An Azure account is primarily used to sign in to the Azure website and administer or deploy services. It is associated with one or more subscriptions and is the entry point for managing Azure services.

132. Answer: B

Explanation: An Azure subscription acts as a logical container used to provision resources such as virtual machines, databases, etc., within Microsoft Azure.

133. Answer: B

Explanation: An Azure subscription has a trust relationship with Microsoft Entra ID, meaning that the subscription trusts Azure AD to authenticate users, services, and devices.

134. Answer: B

Explanation: Each Azure subscription can only trust a single Microsoft Entra ID directory.

135. Answer: C

Explanation: Every Azure subscription includes free access to billing and subscription support, Azure products and services documentation, online self-help documentation, and community support forums.

136. Answer: C

Explanation: An Azure free subscription provides new users with a $200 credit to spend on any service for the first 30 days, free access to the most popular Azure products for 12 months, and access to more than 25 products that are always free.

137. Answer: B

Explanation: To set up a free Azure subscription, you need a phone number, a credit card, and a Microsoft account.

138. Answer: D

Explanation: The Pay-As-You-Go subscription is suitable for a broad spectrum of users, including individuals, small businesses, and large organizations, as it offers a flexible payment plan based on monthly usage.

139. Answer: C

Explanation: Charges in a Pay-As-You-Go subscription are determined monthly based on the services used during that billing period.

140. Answer: D

Explanation: When setting up an Azure Pay-As-You-Go subscription, a user does not need to provide a $200 initial deposit; this is applicable for the Azure free subscription setup.

141. Answer: C

Explanation: The Pay-As-You-Go Dev/Test offer is designed to quickly set up development and testing environments in the cloud, offering pre-configured virtual machines and low rates on various Azure services. This is specifically for teams with Visual Studio subscribers and is limited to development and testing purposes.

142. Answer: B

Explanation: The Pay-As-You-Go Dev/Test offer is exclusively for the development and testing of applications and cannot be used for production environments.

143. Answer: C

Explanation: An Azure Enterprise Agreement provides the flexibility to purchase cloud services and software licenses under one agreement and includes discounts for new licenses, and Software Assurance targeted at enterprise-scale organizations.

144. Answer: B

Explanation: Azure for Students subscription requires verification of student status through an organizational email address to be eligible for the $100 in Azure credits and select free services.

145. Answer: C

Explanation: The Azure for Students subscription includes $100 in Azure credits to be used within the first 12 months and select free services, all without the requirement of a credit card for sign-up.

146. Answer: B

Explanation: Usage within the Pay-As-You-Go Dev/Test subscription does not carry a financially-backed SLA, except for the use of Visual Studio Team Services and HockeyApp.

147. Answer: C

Explanation: You can create multiple subscriptions under a single Azure account, which is particularly useful for businesses as access control and billing are managed at the subscription level.

148. Answer: C

Explanation: Multiple Azure subscriptions provide the benefit of maintaining isolated environments and a separate bill for different projects or teams.

149. Answer: C

Explanation: To sign up for an Azure for Students subscription, you must verify your student status through your organizational email address.

150. Answer: A

Explanation: The Pay-As-You-Go Dev/Test offer includes low rates on virtual machines, Cloud Services, SQL Database, HDInsight, App Service, and Logic Apps, among others.

151. Answer: B

Explanation: Each Azure subscription generates one bill every month, which is automatically charged to the associated account credit or debit card within 10 days after the billing period ends

152. Answer: A

Explanation: Azure AD is for web-based authentication, while Windows AD is for securing Windows desktops and servers. Azure AD supports web-based authentication standards such as OpenID and OAuth.

153. Answer: B

Explanation: A tenant in Microsoft Entra ID (Azure AD) is a dedicated, isolated instance of the Microsoft Entra ID service owned and managed by an organization.

154. Answer: C

Explanation: Yes, a tenant can be associated with multiple Azure subscriptions. However, every subscription is associated with only one tenant.

155. Answer: B

Explanation: If you sign up for Azure with an email address that's not associated with an existing tenant, the sign-up process will guide you through the process of creating a new tenant.

156. Answer: B

Explanation: You can set spending limits on each subscription to manage your spending and avoid surprises at the end of the month

157. Answer: C

Explanation: The line item for an Azure subscription charge on your credit card statement would say MSFT Azure

158. Answer: B

Explanation: Many-to-one: a tenant can be associated with multiple Azure subscriptions, but every subscription is associated with only one tenant

159. Answer: C

Explanation: Reports can be generated by creating separate subscriptions by department or project, which is helpful for internal chargeback purposes

160. Answer: B

Explanation: The account owner of an Azure AD tenant is the original Azure account that is responsible for billing. Additional users can be added to the tenant.

161. Answer: B

Explanation: The Azure ProDirect support plan promises the fastest initial response of one hour or less for high-severity support requests. This is part of their commitment to providing substantial support for mid-size to large companies with critical business operations depending on Azure.

162. Answer: D

Explanation: The Premier support plan is tailored for large or global enterprises and includes the assignment of a Technical Account Manager (TAM) to the account, providing personalized attention and a range of proactive services.

163. Answer: C

Explanation: The Developer plan is designed for non-production environments and offers support for issues with a maximum severity of "C," indicating minimal business impact.

164. Answer: D

Explanation: The Premier support plan provides comprehensive advisory services, including operations and risk assessments, to help enterprises maximize their use of Microsoft platforms and support their business initiatives.

165. Answer: D

Explanation: The Developer support plan is not available to Enterprise customers. They can choose from Standard, Professional Direct, and Premier support plans.

166. Answer: D

Explanation: If a support plan is purchased within a pay-as-you-go subscription, it is charged directly to the monthly Azure subscription bill, making it simple to manage expenses.

Answers

VERSAtile Reads

167. Answer: D

Explanation: The Azure Standard support plan provides guidance and troubleshooting for issues associated with select non-Microsoft technologies running on Azure.

168. Answer: C

Explanation: The Professional Direct support plan includes access to a variety of resources, including "Ask the Experts" webinars, where customers can get insights from Azure specialists.

169. Answer: B

Explanation: The Basic support plan for Microsoft Azure provides billing and subscription support during business hours only, with no mentioned technical support.

170. Answer: B

Explanation: Access to specific preview features is available through the preview features page, where users can select the "Try it" button for the relevant feature they wish to evaluate.

171. Answer: D

Explanation: The Azure portal offers a dashboard view that provides high-level details about the user's Azure environment. This view can be customized by moving and resizing tiles and displaying services of interest.

172. Answer: C

Answers

VERSAtile Reads

Explanation: Azure PowerShell and Azure CLI can be used to automate repetitive tasks by creating administration scripts. Once verified, these scripts can run consistently and help reduce errors.

173. Answer: C

Explanation: Azure Cloud Shell is a web-based command-line interface that allows users to manage Azure resources directly from the browser.

174. Answer: C

Explanation: The 'New-AzureRmVM' command in Azure PowerShell is used to create a new virtual machine within an Azure subscription.

175. Answer: C

Explanation: Before issuing Azure-specific commands in Azure PowerShell, you need to launch PowerShell, install the Azure PowerShell module, and sign in to your Azure account using the command Connect-AzureRMAccount.

176. Answer: B

Explanation: The Azure mobile app is designed for monitoring and managing Azure resources directly from a mobile device.

177. Answer: C

Explanation: Using the Azure portal for complex tasks can be time-consuming and error-prone because it doesn't provide any way to automate repetitive tasks, requiring users to perform actions manually

178. Answer: C

Explanation: The first step is to launch PowerShell and then install the Azure PowerShell module, which provides the necessary commands for managing Azure resources.

179. Answer: C

Explanation: The Azure portal requires users to create VMs one at a time by completing the wizard for each VM, making it inefficient for setting up multiple VMs

180. Answer: B

Explanation: The Azure portal offers a dashboard view that provides high-level details about the user's Azure environment. This view can be customized by moving and resizing tiles and displaying services of interest.

181. Answer: B

Explanation: The Azure CLI is a command-line tool that is used to connect and interact with Azure, allowing users to execute administrative commands on various Azure resources.

182. Answer: C

Explanation: Azure CLI is a cross-platform command-line tool, meaning it can be used on multiple operating systems, including Windows, macOS, and Linux.

183. Answer: B

Explanation: To create a virtual machine using the Azure CLI, you would use the `az vm create` command followed by the appropriate parameters such as resource group and VM name.

184. Answer: B

Explanation: Azure Cloud Shell provides two shell environment options for users: Bash for Linux users and PowerShell for Windows users

185. Answer: D

Explanation: Azure Cloud Shell is a browser-based scripting environment, which allows you to administer Azure resources through a command-line interface from any modern web browser.

186. Answer: B

Explanation: Microsoft Entra ID (Azure AD) is a cloud-based identity and access management service. It helps manage user identities, providing single sign-on (SSO) and multi-factor authentication (MFA) to secure access to applications and resources.

187. Answer: C

Explanation: The Microsoft Azure mobile app is available for both iOS and Android platforms, enabling management of Azure resources from these smartphones and tablets.

188. Answer: A

Explanation: In addition to Azure CLI and Cloud Shell, Azure also provides SDKs for various programming languages and frameworks, as well as REST APIs for programmatic management and control of Azure resources.

189. Answer: B

Explanation: The Azure portal is a web-based administration interface that allows users to manage their Azure subscriptions and interact with the resources they have created.

190. Answer: B

Explanation: When creating a virtual machine using the Azure CLI, you can generate SSH keys by including the `--generate-ssh-keys` parameter in your command, which is helpful for secure remote access to the VM.

191. Answer: D

Explanation: The Azure portal is the primary graphical user interface (GUI) for controlling Microsoft Azure. It is typically the best interface for carrying out single tasks or looking at configuration options in detail.

192. Answer: C

Explanation: A blade in the Azure portal is a slide-out panel that contains the UI for a single level in a navigation sequence. Each subsequent option within a blade can generate another blade to the right, creating a sequence of blades.

193. Answer: C

Explanation: Azure Marketplace allows customers to find, try, purchase, and provision applications and services from hundreds of leading service providers, all certified to run on Azure. It hosts a variety of technical applications and services built for or on Azure.

194. Answer: B

Explanation: At the time of writing, the Azure Marketplace includes over 8,000 listings. It offers a wide range of solutions and services that span several categories.

195. Answer: C

Explanation: Yes, it is possible to test the next version of the Azure portal as it is made available for public preview, allowing users to provide feedback before it becomes generally available

196. Answer: B

Explanation: Azure Policy helps you manage and enforce organizational policies across multiple Azure subscriptions. It ensures compliance by auditing and applying rules to resources.

197. Answer: B

Explanation: If you click the Cloud Shell icon (>_), you will create a new Azure Cloud Shell session. This icon is typically found in the top menu bar of the Azure portal.

198. Answer: D

Explanation: Azure Marketplace's solution catalog spans several industry categories, including open-source container platforms, virtual machine images, databases, application build and deployment software, developer tools, threat detection, blockchain, and more.

199. Answer: D

Explanation: Customers using Azure Marketplace can discover technical applications built for or on Azure, try them, purchase them, and provision or deploy these applications and services in just a few clicks, all within their own Azure environment.

200. Answer: D

Explanation: Azure Marketplace offers a range of products, including SaaS applications, Virtual Machines, Solution Templates, Azure-Managed applications, and consulting services, thereby catering to a wide array of customer needs.

201. Answer: B

Explanation: Azure Compute provides on-demand computing services to run cloud-based applications. It offers resources such as virtual machines and containers to facilitate the running of these applications in the cloud environment.

202. Answer: D

Explanation: Physical servers are not listed as a common technique for computing in Azure. The common techniques are virtual machines, containers, Azure App Service, and serverless computing.

203. Answer: B

Explanation: Virtual machines (VMs) are software emulations of physical computers, including a virtual processor, memory, storage, and networking resources, and they are capable of hosting an operating system and running software like a physical computer.

204. Answer: C

Explanation: Unlike virtual machines, containers do not include a separate operating system for the apps running inside them. Instead, they use the host OS and share its kernel with other containers running on the same host.

205. Answer: C

Explanation: Azure App Service is a platform-as-a-service (PaaS) that is specifically designed to host enterprise-grade web-oriented applications, providing a fully managed platform with performance, scalability, security, and compliance capabilities

206. Answer: C

Explanation: Serverless computing in Azure is a cloud-hosted execution environment that runs your code while abstracting the underlying hosting environment, meaning there's no need for infrastructure configuration or maintenance.

207. Answer: A

Explanation: Azure Resource Manager (ARM) provides a management layer that enables you to create, update, and delete resources in your Azure account. It allows you to manage your infrastructure through declarative templates, rather than scripts, ensuring consistency and automation in the deployment of resources.

208. Answer: D

Explanation: Virtual machines in Azure allow you to use a remote desktop client to use and control the VM as if you were sitting in front of it, due to their emulation of physical computers.

209. Answer: B

Explanation: Containers are used for running applications by bundling the necessary libraries and components without the need for an entire operating system specific to the application. They rely on the host OS.

210. Answer: B

Explanation: Azure Blob Storage is a service designed to store large amounts of unstructured data, such as text and binary data. It is optimized for storing massive amounts of data that is accessed frequently.

211. Answer: B

Explanation: Azure Virtual Machines provide infrastructure as a service (IaaS), allowing users to create and use virtualized servers in the cloud. This enables total control over the operating system and the ability to run custom software and hosting configurations.

212. Answer: C

Explanation: Azure VMs offer Infrastructure as a Service, which means they provide virtualized computing resources over the internet, including virtualized servers with a full OS and the capacity to run custom applications.

213. Answer: A

Explanation: Azure VMs do not provide direct control over the underlying physical hardware but rather provide control over the virtualized environment and the software that runs on it, including the operating system and custom software.

214. Answer: C

Explanation: Similar to a physical computer, you can customize all the software running on an Azure VM, including the operating system and any applications or services you need for your specific use case.

215. Answer: B

Explanation: You can create and provision an Azure VM in minutes, especially when you select a pre-configured VM image, which includes a template with an operating system and possibly other pre-installed software.

216. Answer: B

Explanation: A VM image in Azure is a template that is used to create a virtual machine. It includes an operating system and can also include other pre-installed software that's necessary for the intended use of the VM.

217. Answer: C

Explanation: Selecting an image is crucial when creating a VM because it defines the pre-configured operating system and any additional software that the VM will have, streamlining the setup process for specific use cases.

218. Answer: C

Explanation: Azure Virtual Machines are the ideal choice if you need total control over an operating system, as they provide a virtualized environment where you can fully manage and configure the OS as required.

219. Answer: C

Explanation: Besides offering total control over the operating system, Azure VMs can be used to run custom software and utilize custom hosting configurations, providing flexibility for a wide range of applications.

220. Answer: A

Explanation: Selecting a pre-configured VM image helps bypass the need to manually install the operating system since the image already includes an OS and sometimes other software. This makes the process of deploying a VM faster and more efficient.

221. Answer: B

Explanation: An Availability Set is designed to provide high availability for applications by logically grouping two or more VMs. This helps keep applications available during both planned and unplanned maintenance events by ensuring not all VMs are rebooted at the same time and by automatically switching VMs to a working physical server in case of hardware failures.

222. Answer: C

Explanation: With an Availability Set, you can get up to three fault domains. Each fault domain has a server rack with dedicated power and network resources, providing physical separation and redundancy for your workloads.

223. Answer: C

Explanation: Update domains are used to indicate groups of VMs and underlying physical hardware that can be rebooted at the same time during planned maintenance events. This logical partitioning helps in minimizing downtime.

224. Answer: B

Explanation: An unplanned maintenance event involves hardware failure in the data center, such as a power outage or disk failure, and is distinct from planned maintenance events, which are scheduled updates to the Azure fabric.

225. Answer: D

Explanation: An Availability Set provides five logical update domains, which are part of the Azure data center's logical architecture to manage VM reboots during updates without impacting the entire set at once.

226. Answer: C

Explanation: Virtual Machine Scale Sets are used to create and manage a group of identical, load-balanced VMs that can automatically scale in response to demand or a defined schedule, allowing for the management of large-scale services.

227. Answer: C

Explanation: A Virtual Machine Scale Set can automatically create and integrate with Azure load balancer or Application Gateway to balance and distribute traffic across multiple VM instances.

228. Answer: B

Explanation: There is no additional cost for the management and automation features that scale sets provide, such as auto-scale and redundancy. You only pay for the underlying compute resources.

229. Answer: C

Explanation: Virtual Machine Scale Sets automatically distribute VM instances across Availability Zones or Availability Sets, ensuring high availability and redundancy for your applications.

230. Answer: D

Explanation: In a manual group of VMs, adding additional VM instances is a manual process where each VM needs to be created, configured, and ensured compliance. In contrast, VM Scale Sets allow for automatic creation from a central configuration.

231. Answer: C

Explanation: Azure Batch is designed for large-scale job scheduling and compute management, allowing users to scale to tens, hundreds, or thousands of VMs. It automates the process of starting to compute VMs, installing applications, running jobs, handling failures, queuing work, and scaling down resources once the work is completed.

232. Answer: B

Explanation: Azure Batch is not involved in email server configuration. It is focused on compute management, including starting VMs, managing applications, job execution, failure handling, and queuing tasks.

233. Answer: C

Explanation: Containers are lightweight and provide secure, isolated environments to run multiple instances of applications on a single VM host, saving resources and allowing for easier management.

234. Answer: B

Explanation: Azure Container Instances (ACI) is the fastest and simplest PaaS offering in Azure to run containers, eliminating the need to manage virtual machines or additional services.

235. Answer: D

Explanation: Azure Kubernetes Service (AKS) provides a complete orchestration service for containers, automating and managing a large number of containers in distributed architectures.

236. Answer: A

Explanation: Azure supports Docker containers primarily through Azure Container Instances (ACI) and Azure Kubernetes Service (AKS), which are dedicated services for container management and orchestration

237. Answer: B

Explanation: Containers are often used to create solutions using a micro-service architecture, where applications are broken down into smaller, independent components that can be managed and scaled separately.

238. Answer: B

Explanation: In a micro-service architecture, a website can be split into different containers for each logical section, such as the front end, back end, and storage, allowing each part to be maintained and scaled independently.

239. Answer: C

Explanation: Azure Container Instances (ACI) is a PaaS offering that allows users to run containers directly without the overhead of managing virtual machines or additional services

240. Answer: B

Explanation: Container orchestration in Azure, particularly through Azure Kubernetes Service (AKS), helps in automating and managing container deployment, scaling, and management within distributed architectures.

241. Answer: C

Explanation: Containers are designed to be lightweight and can be created, scaled out, and stopped dynamically, which allows for quick responses to changes in demand or failure. They also enable multiple isolated applications to run on a single VM host without the need for separate VMs for each app.

242. Answer: C

Explanation: Azure App Service is a platform-as-a-service (PaaS) offering that enables developers to build, deploy, and manage applications without worrying about the underlying infrastructure. It supports a variety of programming languages and frameworks.

243. Answer: C

Explanation: Azure Kubernetes Service (AKS) is a comprehensive orchestration service that automates and manages the interaction with a large number of containers, particularly useful in distributed architectures with multiple containers

244. Answer: C

Explanation: A micro-service architecture involves breaking down solutions into smaller, independent pieces that can be maintained, scaled, or updated independently. Containers are ideally suited for this as they can host these pieces, like a front end, back end, or storage, in separate isolated environments.

245. Answer: B

Explanation: Azure App Service is a platform as a service (PaaS) that enables users to build and host web apps, background jobs, mobile backend, and RESTful APIs without managing the underlying infrastructure.

246. Answer: D

Explanation: Azure App Service provides full support for hosting web apps using a variety of programming languages, including ASP.NET, ASP.NET Core, Java, Ruby, Node.js, PHP, and Python.

247. Answer: B

Explanation: Azure API Apps allow developers to build REST-based Web APIs using their choice of programming language and framework, with full Swagger support for easier documentation and client generation.

248. Answer: B

Explanation: Azure WebJobs enables you to run programs or scripts as background tasks in the same context as a web app, API app, or mobile app. These tasks can be scheduled or triggered based on certain conditions.

249. Answer: C

Explanation: Azure App Service supports both Windows and Linux as host operating systems for web apps, giving developers the flexibility to choose an environment that best suits their application requirements.

250. Answer: C

Explanation: Azure App Service handles deployment and infrastructure management for web apps, allowing developers to focus on the application logic. At the same time, Azure takes care of the necessary infrastructure to run and scale the web applications.

251. Answer: C

Explanation: The Mobile Apps feature of Azure App Service is specifically designed to help quickly build a back-end for iOS and Android apps. It allows for storing data in a cloud-based SQL database, authenticating customers, sending push notifications, and executing custom back-end logic.

252. Answer: B

Explanation: Azure Functions can execute code in almost any modern language, scaling automatically based on demand, which makes them ideal for services where you are only concerned about the code.

253. Answer: C

Explanation: With serverless computing in Azure, you are billed only for the exact resources you use. There is no need to reserve capacity ahead of time.

254. Answer: C

Explanation: Durable Functions are stateful versions of Azure Functions that pass context through the function to keep track of prior activity.

255. Answer: C

Explanation: Azure Logic Apps are designed to automate your business processes using workflows built from predefined logic blocks in a visual designer

256. Answer: C

Explanation: Azure Logic Apps provide over 200 different connectors and processing blocks to interact with various services, including the most popular enterprise apps.

257. Answer: B

Explanation: Workflows in Azure Logic Apps can be created using a visual designer available on the Azure Portal or in Visual Studio, which is then persisted as a JSON file.

258. Answer: B

Explanation: By default, Azure Functions are stateless and behave as if they are restarted every time they respond to an event.

259. Answer: C

Explanation: Serverless apps in Azure are configured to respond to events, such as a REST endpoint, a periodic timer, or a message received from another Azure service, and they run only when triggered by such an event.

260. Answer: A

Explanation: With the Mobile Apps feature, you can execute custom back-end logic in C# or Node.js, among other capabilities like data storage, authentication, and push notifications.

261. Answer: B

Explanation: Azure Event Grid is designed for event-driven reactive programming. It uses a publish-subscribe model to route events efficiently and reliably from Azure and non-Azure resources, allowing for reactive programming patterns.

262. Answer: D

Explanation: Azure Event Hubs are ideal for big data pipeline scenarios as they facilitate the capture, retention, and replay of telemetry and event stream data from many concurrent sources.

263. Answer: B

Explanation: Azure Service Bus is intended for high-value enterprise messaging where features such as transactions, ordering, duplicate detection, and instantaneous consistency are crucial.

264. Answer: C

Explanation: Event loops are not a concept in Azure Event Grid. The concepts include events, event sources, topics, event subscriptions, and event handlers.

265. Answer: C

Explanation: Durable Functions are an extension of Azure Functions that enable stateful functions in a serverless environment.

266. Answer: B

Explanation: Azure Key Vault is a cloud service that provides secure storage and management of sensitive information, such as secrets, keys, and certificates. It helps you safeguard cryptographic keys and secrets used by cloud applications and services.

267. Answer: B

Explanation: Azure Logic Apps uses a designer-first (declarative) approach where you define the actions and their relationships using a GUI.

268. Answer: C

Explanation: Azure Functions allows you to run your code locally or in the cloud, providing flexibility in deployment and testing.

269. Answer: C

Explanation: Event subscriptions in Azure Event Grid are used to route events to the correct event handler, and they can intelligently filter incoming events as required.

270. Answer: C

Explanation: Azure Service Bus is designed for applications that require reliable state transition management for business processes, which is often needed in traditional enterprise applications.

271. Answer: B

Explanation: Azure IoT solutions are designed to connect, monitor, and control billions of IoT assets. These solutions are a collection of Microsoft-managed cloud services that enable communication between IoT devices and back-end services running in the cloud.

272. Answer: D

Explanation: Mobile applications are not considered a main component of an IoT solution. The core components of an IoT solution include devices, back-end services, and communications between the two.

273. Answer: B

Explanation: Azure IoT Central is a SaaS (Software as a Service) solution that helps users connect, monitor, and manage IoT devices. It provides templates for device types and allows for the creation of IoT Central applications for device operators.

274. Answer: B

Explanation: IoT solution accelerators are a collection of PaaS (Platform as a Service) solutions that provide templates to help accelerate the development of an IoT solution. These accelerators allow for customization to meet specific requirements.

275. Answer: C

Explanation: Azure Digital Twins enables users to create comprehensive models of the physical environment, including the relationships and interactions between people, spaces, and devices.

276. Answer: B

Explanation The IoT Hub Device Provisioning Service is a helper service for IoT Hub that allows secure and rapid provisioning of devices to an IoT hub, which can be done on a large scale.

277. Answer: B

Explanation: IoT Edge is a service that enables data analysis to occur directly on IoT devices (at the "edge"), reducing the need for data to be sent to the cloud for analysis.

278. Answer: B

Explanation: Azure Maps provides geographic information to web and mobile applications. It includes REST APIs and a web-based JavaScript control for creating applications with mapping capabilities.

279. Answer: B

Explanation: A back-end service could request a device to send telemetry, such as temperature data from a mobile refrigeration truck, more frequently to help diagnose a problem.

280. Answer: B

Explanation: Time Series Insights is the service that enables the storage, visualization, and querying of large amounts of time series data generated by IoT devices, which can be used in conjunction with IoT Hub.

281. Answer: B

Explanation: Azure IoT Central is a fully managed IoT software-as-a-service solution that facilitates the creation of products that connect the physical and digital worlds, thereby enabling better products and experiences for customers.

282. Answer: D

Explanation: Azure IoT Solution Accelerators provide prebuilt solutions like remote monitoring, connected factory, predictive maintenance, and device simulation, but they do not specifically include mobile app development.

283. Answer: B

Explanation: Azure IoT Hub is a managed service that serves as a central message hub for bi-directional communication between IoT applications and the devices they manage.

284. Answer: B

Explanation: Azure Stream Analytics is a real-time analytics and complex event-processing engine designed to analyze and process high volumes of fast streaming data from multiple sources, including telemetry streams from IoT devices.

285. Answer: C

Explanation: IoT Hub supports multiple messaging patterns, including device-to-cloud telemetry for sending data from devices to the cloud and cloud-to-device messages for sending commands and policies from the cloud to devices.

286. Answer: B

Explanation: Azure IoT Edge is a service that allows data analysis on devices, or "at the edge," to minimize communication with the cloud and react more quickly to events.

287. Answer: B

Explanation: Azure Digital Twins enables the creation of comprehensive models of the physical environment, including the interactions between people, spaces, and devices, for predictive maintenance and other advanced analyses.

288. Answer: B

Explanation: The IoT Hub Device Provisioning Service assists IoT Hub by enabling secure and scalable zero-touch, just-in-time provisioning of devices to the appropriate IoT hub without human intervention.

289. Answer: B

Explanation: The Basic tier of IoT Hub is intended for solutions that only need unidirectional communication from devices to the cloud, whereas the Standard tier enables bi-directional communication, including cloud-to-device messaging

290. Answer: C

Explanation: Azure IoT Central allows for easy customization of applications, working with industry-leading technologies such as Azure IoT Hub, which is the underlying service for IoT Central and IoT solution accelerators.

291. Answer: C

Explanation: Azure Time Series Insights is designed for storing, visualizing, and querying large amounts of time series data generated by IoT devices. It allows integration with IoT Hub and helps in managing the data effectively.

292. Answer: B

Explanation: Azure Maps provides geographic information to web and mobile applications. It offers a set of REST APIs and a web-based JavaScript control that can be used to develop applications for various platforms, including Apple and Windows devices.

293. Answer: C

Explanation: Machine learning in Azure Fundamentals is a technique that allows computers to use existing data to forecast future behaviors, outcomes, and trends without being explicitly programmed. It is used to make applications and devices smarter by providing predictive capabilities.

294. Answer: C

Explanation: Azure Machine Learning service fully supports open-source technologies such as PyTorch, TensorFlow, and scikit-learn. It provides a versatile environment for various types of machine learning, including classical machine learning, deep learning, and supervised and unsupervised learning.

295. Answer: C

Explanation: Azure Machine Learning Studio offers an interactive, visual workspace where users can build, test, and iterate on a predictive analysis model using a drag-and-drop approach. This enables users to construct their models without the need for programming.

296. Answer: B

Explanation: A key difference is that Machine Learning Studio uses proprietary compute targets for training, whereas Azure Machine Learning service uses the user's computing resources. Additionally, the service is fully integrated into Azure and provides both SDKs and a visual interface.

297. Answer: B

Explanation: Azure Machine Learning Studio supports a proprietary compute target with CPU support only for training models. This is a limitation compared to Azure Machine Learning service, which allows the use of the user's computing resources.

298. Answer: C

Explanation: Automated model training and hyper-parameter tuning are not available in Azure Machine Learning Studio. These features are available in the Azure Machine Learning service.

299. Answer: B

Explanation: Azure Databricks is an Apache Spark-based analytics platform optimized for the Microsoft Azure cloud services platform. It is designed to provide streamlined workflows and interactive workspaces for collaboration among various roles in data analytics.

300. Answer: A

Explanation: Azure Databricks can read data from multiple data sources, including Azure Blob Storage, Azure Data Lake Storage, Azure Cosmos DB, and Azure SQL Data Warehouse, to turn it into insights using Spark. This capability is part of its big data pipeline functionality.

301. Answer: C

Explanation: Azure data storage ensures data security through encryption capabilities. This means data is encrypted to make it highly secure, and users have tight control over who can access the data.

302. Answer: D

Explanation: Azure can store a variety of data types, including video files, text files, and large binary files like virtual hard disks, as well as relational and NoSQL data.

303. Answer: D

Explanation: Azure has the capability of storing up to 8 TB of data in its virtual disks, which is significant for storing heavy data such as videos and simulations.

304. Answer: B

Explanation: Azure employs storage tiers to prioritize access to data, differentiating between frequently used information and rarely used information.

305. Answer: C

Explanation: Structured data in Azure Storage refers to data that follows a specific schema, where all data has the same fields or properties and is typically stored in database tables with rows and columns.

306. Answer: C

Explanation: Azure data storage includes replication across multiple global locations to protect against both planned events, like scheduled maintenance, and unplanned events, such as hardware failures.

307. Answer: C

Explanation: Semi-structured data does not fit neatly into rows and columns; instead, it uses tags or keys to organize the data and provide a hierarchy.

308. Answer: D

Explanation: Unstructured data encompasses data that has no designated structure, meaning there are no restrictions on the kinds of data it can hold, which can include PDF documents, images, JSON files, video content, etc.

309. Answer: B

Explanation: Automated backup and recovery are significant features of Azure data storage that mitigate the risk of data loss due to unforeseen failures or interruptions

310. **Answer: C**

Explanation: Structured data relies on keys to indicate how one row in a table relates to data in another row of another table, adhering to a relational model

311. **Answer: C**

Explanation: Azure SQL Database is a relational database as a service (DaaS) based on the latest stable version of the Microsoft SQL Server database engine. It offers high-performance reliability and is a fully managed and secure database.

312. **Answer: B**

Explanation: Azure Database Migration Service uses the Data Migration Assistant to generate assessment reports that provide recommendations to guide users through the changes required before performing a migration.

313. **Answer: C**

Explanation: Azure SQL Data Warehouse uses Massively Parallel Processing (MPP) to quickly run complex queries across petabytes of data.

314. **Answer: B**

Explanation: SQL Data Warehouse acts as a key component of a big data solution, with the capability to run high-performance analytics on large volumes of data.

315. **Answer: B**

Explanation: SQL Data Warehouse integrates big data into the warehouse by using simple PolyBase T-SQL queries, which enables the analysis of large volumes of data

316. **Answer: C**

Explanation: SQL Data Warehouse stores data in relational tables with columnar storage, which significantly reduces data storage costs and improves query performance.

317. Answer: B

Explanation: The outcome of running analytics on SQL Data Warehouse is that it becomes the single version of truth your business can rely on for insights.

318. Answer: C

Explanation: When using SQL Data Warehouse, analysis queries can finish in seconds instead of minutes or hours instead of days, representing a significant performance improvement over traditional database systems.

319. Answer: B

Explanation: The analysis results from SQL Data Warehouse can be directed to worldwide reporting databases or applications, facilitating widespread access to business insights.

320. Answer: B

Explanation: The key benefit for business analysts using SQL Data Warehouse is the ability to gain insights that lead to well-informed business decisions

321. Answer: A

Explanation: Azure Cosmos DB is Microsoft's globally distributed, multi-model database service designed to provide low latency, high availability, and elastic scalability for applications worldwide.

322. Answer: B

Explanation: Azure Cosmos DB supports multiple APIs for data access, including SQL, MongoDB, Cassandra, Tables, or Gremlin, making it a versatile choice for various data models.

323. Answer: B

Explanation: Azure Storage is Microsoft's cloud solution designed for modern data storage scenarios, offering a range of services like object storage, file system service, messaging store, and NoSQL store.

324. Answer: D

Explanation: Azure Blob storage is optimized for storing massive amounts of unstructured data such as text, binary data, images, and video.

325. Answer: B

Explanation: Objects in Azure Blob storage can be accessed from anywhere in the world via HTTP/HTTPS, providing a high level of accessibility.

326. Answer: C

Explanation: Azure Storage client libraries are available for a variety of programming languages, including .NET, Java, Node.js, Python, Go, PHP, and Ruby.

327. Answer: B

Explanation: Azure Queues provides a messaging store for reliable messaging between application components, ensuring communication within distributed applications.

328. Answer: B

Explanation: Azure Tables is a service within Azure Storage that offers a NoSQL store for schema-less storage of structured data.

329. Answer: C

Explanation: Azure Cosmos DB achieves low latency and high availability by deploying instances in multiple data centers worldwide, thus being close to the users and reducing response time.

330. Answer: A and C

Explanation: Azure Blob Storage is suitable for storing data for backup and restore, disaster recovery, archiving, and streaming video and audio content. It is not used for relational database management or messaging between application components.

331. Answer: C

Explanation: Azure Data Lake Storage Gen2 is designed to act as the foundation for building enterprise data lakes on Azure, capable of handling multiple petabytes of information and sustaining hundreds of gigabits of throughput.

332. Answer: B

Explanation: A data lake is a large repository that holds a vast pool of raw data, the purpose for which is not yet defined, while a data warehouse is a repository for structured, filtered data that has already been processed for a specific purpose.

333. Answer: A

Explanation: Data Lake Storage Gen2 introduces a hierarchical namespace that organizes objects/files into a hierarchy of directories for efficient data access, unlike the traditional object-based access mode that stores objects in a flat model.

334. Answer: C

Explanation: With the addition of a hierarchical namespace in Data Lake Storage Gen2, operations such as renaming or deleting a directory are simplified into single atomic metadata operations rather than processing all objects that share the name prefix of the directory.

335. Answer: B

Explanation: Azure HDInsight and Azure Databricks are tools specifically mentioned for running data analysis jobs on data stored in Data Lake Storage Gen2 due to their capabilities to handle big data analytics workloads.

336. Answer: B

Explanation: Azure Data Lake Analytics is an on-demand analytics job service that simplifies big data by eliminating the need for configuring and tuning hardware. Users write queries to transform data and extract insights and only pay for the job when it is running.

337. Answer: B

Explanation: Azure HDInsight is a cloud service that facilitates easy, fast, and cost-effective processing of massive amounts of data through a managed, full-spectrum, open-source analytics service for enterprises.

338. Answer: B

Explanation: Azure Data Lake is likened to a large container, similar to a lake with rivers of data flowing into it, signifying the inflow of various types of data from multiple sources.

339. Answer: D

Explanation: Azure Data Lake is versatile in its storage capabilities, able to store a massive variety of data types, including structured and unstructured data, log files, real-time data, images, and more.

340. Answer: B

Explanation: Azure HDInsight is used for processing large volumes of data using big data frameworks such as Hadoop and Spark, which are supported in HDInsight clusters.

341. Answer: C

Explanation: Azure Files uses the Server Message Block (SMB) protocol to enable file access, which allows multiple VMs to share the same files with read and write access.

342. Answer: B

Explanation: Azure Files can be accessed from anywhere by using a URL that points to the file and includes a shared access signature (SAS) token, which allows specified access to a private asset for a certain amount of time.

343. Answer: B

Explanation: Azure Files is commonly used for migrating on-premises applications that utilize file shares to Azure with minimal changes.

344. Answer: B

Explanation: Azure Queue Storage is a service for storing large numbers of messages and provides asynchronous message queueing for communication between application components.

345. Answer: C

Explanation: Azure Queue Storage offers asynchronous message queueing, which can help distribute the load among different web servers and manage bursts of traffic.

346. Answer: C

Explanation: Azure-managed disks are stored as page blobs, which are random IO storage objects in Azure.

347. Answer: B

Explanation: In the context of Azure-managed disks, 'managed' means that Azure abstracts over page blobs, blob containers, and storage accounts, taking care of the management automatically.

348. Answer: C

Explanation: Azure Disk Storage is designed to provide persistent, high-performance storage for Azure virtual machines (VMs). It offers various types of disks (such as Standard HDD, Standard SSD, and Premium SSD) to meet different performance and price needs. This type of storage is crucial for VMs because it retains data even when the VM is powered off, restarted, or deallocated, ensuring that the data is always available when the VM is running. This makes Azure Disk Storage the optimal choice for applications requiring reliable, high-performance storage solutions. Hence, the typical use case for Azure Disk Storage is persistent data storage for VMs.

349. Answer: A

Explanation: Azure Files can be used for storing configuration files on a file share and accessing them from multiple VMs.

350. Answer: C

Explanation: By decoupling application components using Azure Queue Storage, you can build resilience against component failure when multiple users access your data at the same time.

351. Answer: C

Explanation: Azure Table storage is primarily used for storing structured NoSQL data in the cloud. It provides a key/attribute store with a schema-less design, making it suitable for flexible datasets like user data for web applications, address books, device information, and other types of metadata required by services.

352. Answer: B

Explanation: The OData protocol and LINQ queries can be used to access data in Azure Table storage. This enables fast querying of data using a clustered index and access through WCF Data Service .NET Libraries.

353. Answer: C

Explanation: You should consider using Azure Blobs when you want to store unstructured data at a massive scale and perform big data analytics, specifically with Azure Data Lake Storage Gen2 solutions.

354. Answer: B

Explanation: Azure Files provides an SMB (Server Message Block) interface. It is useful for "lift and shift" scenarios because it allows applications that already use native file system APIs to share data easily between them and other applications running in Azure.

355. Answer: C

Explanation: The hot storage tier is optimized for data that is accessed frequently. It has higher storage costs but lower access costs and is ideal for data in active use or expected to be accessed often.

356. Answer: B

Explanation: The cool access tier is intended for data that is infrequently accessed and is recommended to be stored for at least 30 days.

357. Answer: B

Explanation: For blobs in the archive access tier, the valid operations include GetBlobProperties, GetBlobMetadata, ListBlobs, SetBlobTier, and DeleteBlob. Data retrieval has higher latency, and snapshots cannot be taken.

358. Answer: C

Explanation: Azure Storage Service Encryption (SSE) provides security for data at rest by encrypting the data before storing it and decrypting it before retrieval.

359. Answer: B

Explanation: Data replication is the term used to describe the process of ensuring data is durable and always available in Azure. Azure provides regional and geographic replications to protect data against various disasters.

360. Answer: B

Explanation: Azure Disk storage is most appropriate for "lift and shift" scenarios where applications use native file system APIs to read and write data to persistent disks. It allows data to be persistently stored and accessed from an attached virtual hard disk.

361. Answer: B

Explanation: Azure Virtual Network (VNet) is meant to enable Azure resources to securely communicate with each other, the internet, and on-premises networks. It is the fundamental building block for your private network in Azure, which allows the deployment of VMs and other Azure resources within a secure and private network space.

362. Answer: B

Explanation: Azure ExpressRoute is used to extend your on-premises networks into the Microsoft Cloud over a private connection facilitated by a connectivity provider. It offers a more reliable and faster connection compared to traditional internet connections.

363. Answer: C

Explanation: Azure Virtual WAN (Virtual Wide Area Network) is a networking service that provides optimized and automated branch connectivity to and through Azure. Azure regions serve as hubs to which branches can connect, leveraging the Azure backbone.

364. Answer: D

Explanation: Virtual networks (VNets) can be connected using virtual network peering, enabling resources in either virtual network to communicate with each other. This can be done within the same or different Azure regions.

365. Answer: C

Explanation: Azure DNS is used to host DNS domains that provide name resolution by using Microsoft Azure infrastructure, ensuring that your domain's DNS queries are answered by Azure's global network of DNS servers.

366. Answer: B

Explanation: Azure Bastion provides secure and seamless RDP/SSH connectivity to your virtual machines directly in the Azure portal over SSL. When connecting through Azure Bastion, the virtual machines do not require a public IP address, enhancing security.

367. Answer: B

Explanation: Resources in Azure Virtual Network can communicate inbound to the internet by assigning a public IP address or using a public Load Balancer. This allows resources to be accessible from the internet while maintaining control over inbound connections.

368. Answer: B

Explanation: VPN Gateway is the service that sends encrypted traffic between an Azure virtual network and an on-premises location over the public Internet. This ensures secure communications using encryption.

369. Answer: D

Explanation: You can connect your on-premises computers and networks to a virtual network using VPN Gateway or ExpressRoute to enable them to communicate with the virtual network. This provides a way to extend your local network into the Azure cloud.

370. Answer: D

Explanation: Azure Traffic Manager falls under the category of application delivery services. It is used to deliver applications in the Azure network by directing client requests to the most appropriate service endpoint based on traffic-routing methods and health probes.

371. Answer: B

Explanation: Azure DDoS protection is designed to safeguard applications by maintaining their high availability and protecting them from distributed denial-of-service attacks, which can cause excess IP traffic charges and service disruption

372. Answer: A

Explanation: Azure Front Door Service provides global routing for web traffic with an emphasis on performance optimization and instant global failover, ensuring high availability for applications.

373. Answer: C

Explanation: Azure Firewall is a cloud-based security service that acts as a fully stateful firewall to protect Azure Virtual Network resources.

374. Answer: C

Explanation: Azure Load Balancer is designed to provide regional load-balancing by routing traffic within virtual networks (VNets), balancing traffic across and between resources in a region.

375. Answer: C

Explanation: Azure Traffic Manager uses DNS to redirect requests to the best endpoint based on geographical location without actually seeing the traffic passing between the client and the service.

376. Answer: C

Explanation: N-tier architectures, such as the three-tier architecture used in e-commerce applications, separate concerns into logical tiers that can be independently updated, replaced, or even expanded with new tiers as needed.

377. Answer: B

Explanation: Azure Application Gateway is a web traffic load balancer that enables the management of traffic to web applications, applying routing rules for layer-7 (HTTP) load balancing.

378. Answer: C

Explanation: Azure Network Watcher provides tools to monitor and diagnose connectivity issues, including VPN, NSG, and routing issues, as well as the ability to capture packets on VMs.

379. Answer: C

Explanation: Azure's Content Delivery Network (CDN) minimizes latency in delivering high-bandwidth content to users by storing cached content on edge servers in point-of-presence (POP) locations that are close to the end-users.

380. Answer: C

Explanation: An Azure Region refers to a set of data centers deployed within a latency-defined perimeter and connected through a dedicated regional low-latency network. Common examples include East US, West US, and North Europe.

381. Answer: C

Explanation: A virtual network in Azure is a logically isolated network that is scoped to a single region, allowing Azure resources to communicate securely with each other, the internet, and on-premises networks.

382. Answer: B

Explanation: Multiple virtual networks from different regions can be connected using virtual network peering, allowing them to communicate with each other as if they were part of the same network

383. Answer: C

Explanation: Subnets enable you to segment a virtual network into one or more sub-networks and allocate a portion of the virtual network's address space to each subnet, improving address allocation efficiency and organization within the network.

384. Answer: C

Explanation: A VPN gateway is a type of virtual network gateway in Azure that enables a secure connection between an Azure Virtual Network and an on-premises location over the internet.

385. Answer: B

Explanation: Each virtual network in Azure can have only one VPN gateway, though you can create multiple connections to the same VPN gateway.

386. Answer: C

Explanation: You configure virtual networks and gateways through software in Azure, which allows you to treat a virtual network just like your own network.

387. Answer: C

Explanation: A Network Security Group (NSG) acts as a cloud-level firewall for your network, allowing or denying inbound traffic to your Azure resources based on the rules you set.

388. Answer: B

Explanation: Network Security Groups can be configured to accept traffic only from known sources, such as IP addresses that you trust, which improves the security of your virtual network.

389. Answer: B

Explanation: The VM in the web tier allows inbound traffic on ports 22 (SSH) and 80 (HTTP), as indicated by the network security group settings described in the context.

390. Answer: B

Explanation: With a virtual network in Azure, you can choose which networks your virtual network can reach, including the public internet or other networks within the private IP address space.

391. Answer: B

Explanation: High Availability aims at ensuring that critical systems are always operational. It involves creating mechanisms for automatic failover and eliminating single points of failure to achieve long periods of uninterrupted service.

392. Answer: B

Explanation: Fault Tolerance describes a system designed to immediately hand over operations to a backup component with no loss of service when a failure occurs, ensuring continuity of operations.

.393. Answer: B

Explanation: The key distinction is that Fault Tolerance ensures the continuation and correct completion of an action when a failure occurs. High Availability does not guarantee the end state of the action in progress but ensures the system remains responsive to new requests.

394. Answer A

Explanation: A Load Balancer is used to evenly distribute incoming traffic among multiple systems, helping to achieve both high availability and resiliency. It serves as the entry point to the user and facilitates maintenance without service interruption.

395. Answer: B

Explanation: Disaster Recovery (DR) is a strategic approach aimed at ensuring that an organization can quickly resume mission-critical functions following a disaster or disruptive event. This can include natural disasters, cyber-attacks, equipment failures, or other unexpected incidents. DR involves a combination of planning, policies, procedures, and technologies designed to protect an organization's IT infrastructure and data. The primary goal is to minimize downtime and data loss, thereby maintaining business continuity. Therefore, the purpose of Disaster Recovery is to ensure the continuity and recovery of systems after a disruptive event.

396. Answer: B

Explanation: A Load Balancer can detect when a system (e.g., a virtual machine) is unresponsive due to maintenance and can redirect traffic to other systems in the pool, thereby allowing maintenance to occur without interrupting the service.

397. Answer: B

Explanation: Redundancy refers to the concept of having backup components in place so that if one fails, another can take over immediately. This is essential for achieving Fault Tolerance.

398. Answer: D

Explanation: Resiliency refers to a system's ability to stay operational during various abnormal conditions, including natural disasters, maintenance, traffic spikes, and threats from malicious parties.

399. Answer: C

Explanation: Disaster Recovery goes beyond the capabilities of High Availability and Fault Tolerance by offering a comprehensive strategy for recovering from major disasters that can cause extensive downtime.

400. Answer: C

Explanation: During maintenance, if a Load Balancer detects that a VM is unresponsive, it will direct incoming traffic to other responsive VMs in the pool to ensure continuous service.

401. Answer: C

Explanation: Infrastructure as a Service (IaaS) is the Azure service level where the user is responsible for patching and securing operating systems and software. This service provides virtual machines and virtual networks that the user must maintain.

402. Answer: B

Explanation: In a PaaS offering, Azure manages the operating system and most of the foundational software, such as database management systems. This includes updating them with the latest security patches.

403. Answer: B

Explanation: PaaS provides operational advantages by allowing users to "point and click" within the Azure portal or run automated scripts to deploy complex, secured systems easily and scale them as needed

404. Answer: C

Explanation: Contoso Shipping uses Azure Event Hubs for ingesting telemetry data from drones and trucks, which is an example of PaaS

405. Answer: B

Explanation: The primary goal of a defense-in-depth strategy is to employ a series of mechanisms that can slow the advance of an attack aimed at acquiring unauthorized access to information, thus protecting the data

406. Answer: B

Explanation: The defense in depth strategy is visualized as a set of concentric rings, with the data at the center, each ring adding a layer of security around the data

407. Answer: C

Explanation: In most cases, attackers are after data, which can be stored in various forms like databases, virtual machines, SaaS applications, or cloud storage. The defense-in-depth strategy aims to protect this data.

408. Answer: B

Explanation: An Azure Cosmos DB backend in a web app is an example of a Platform as a Service (PaaS), where Azure manages the operating system, database management systems, and other foundational software

409. Answer: C

Explanation: Software as a Service (SaaS) outsources almost everything, including the software and internet infrastructure. The software is controlled by the vendor but configured for the customer's use.

410. Answer: C

Explanation: Regulatory requirements often dictate the controls and processes that must be in place to ensure the confidentiality, integrity, and availability of data

411. Answer: C

Explanation: The primary focus of the compute layer is ensuring that compute resources are secure. This includes securing access to virtual machines, implementing endpoint protection, and keeping systems patched and current to prevent malware, unpatched systems, and improperly secured systems from opening the environment to attacks.

412. Answer: B

Explanation: By limiting the network connectivity across all resources to only what is required, you reduce the risk of lateral movement throughout your network. This helps in enhancing security by controlling the flow of traffic and potential pathways that could be exploited for unauthorized access.

413. Answer: B

Explanation: At the perimeter layer, using DDoS protection is important to filter large-scale attacks before they can cause a denial of service for end-users. Additionally, using perimeter firewalls helps identify and alert to malicious attacks against your network.

414. Answer: C

Explanation: Controlling access to infrastructure and implementing change control is crucial. Using single sign-on and multi-factor authentication, as well as auditing events and changes, ensures that identities are secure, access is appropriately granted, and changes are logged for security and compliance purposes.

415. Answer: C

Explanation: Physical security measures are intended to provide physical safeguards against unauthorized access to assets, ensuring that other security layers can't be bypassed and handling loss or theft appropriately. It serves as the first line of defense in a comprehensive security strategy.

Answers

416. Answer: B

Explanation: Implementing endpoint protection helps keep systems secure from malware as it provides security measures directly on the endpoints (such as user devices and servers), which includes antivirus, anti-malware, and personal firewalls.

417. Answer: A

Explanation: Restricting inbound internet access helps minimize security risks by controlling the potential entry points for external threats. While necessary connections should be maintained, unnecessary inbound access should be limited to reduce exposure to attacks.

418. Answer: B

Explanation: Multi-factor authentication reinforces identity and access security by requiring multiple forms of verification before granting access to a system or application. This adds a layer of defense against unauthorized access.

419. Answer: B

Explanation: Implementing DDoS protection at the network perimeter filters out large-scale attacks, such as distributed denial of service attacks, before they can overwhelm the network and cause a denial of service for end-users. This helps ensure availability and continuity of services.

420. Answer: B

Explanation: Auditing events and changes is important for compliance and security as it provides a record of who accessed what resources and when, as well as what changes were made. This transparency helps in detecting unauthorized activities and aids in investigations after security incidents.

421. Answer: B

Explanation: Data in transit refers to data that is actively moving from one location to another, such as across the internet or through a private network. It is important to encrypt this data to protect it from outside observers and to reduce the risk of exposure during transmission.

422. Answer: C

Explanation: Azure Storage Service Encryption (SSE) automatically encrypts data before persisting it to Azure Managed Disks, Azure Blob storage, Azure Files, or Azure Queue storage, and decrypts the data before retrieval. This process is transparent to applications using these services.

423. Answer: C

Explanation: Azure Disk Encryption (ADE) leverages the industry-standard BitLocker feature for Windows virtual machine disks and dm-crypt for Linux virtual machine disks to provide volume encryption.

424. Answer: D

Explanation: Transparent Data Encryption (TDE) helps protect Azure SQL Database and Azure Data Warehouse by performing real-time encryption and decryption of the database, associated backups, and transaction log files at rest without requiring changes to the application.

425. Answer: C

Explanation: By default, Azure provides a unique encryption key per logical SQL Server instance for Transparent Data Encryption and handles all the details of encryption.

426. Answer: C

Explanation: Azure Key Vault is a centralized cloud service for storing application secrets, keys, and certificates. It helps control access to these secrets and provides secure access, permissions control, and access logging capabilities.

427. Answer: C

Explanation: Azure Key Vault can be used to securely store and tightly control access to tokens, passwords, certificates, API keys, and other secrets.

428. Answer: C

Explanation: Azure Key Vault allows storing secrets and keys either by using software or by FIPS 140-2 Level 2 validated Hardware Security Modules (HSMs).

429. Answer: C

Explanation: Centralizing storage for application secrets in Azure Key Vault allows control over their distribution and reduces the chances that secrets may be accidentally leaked.

430. Answer: C

Explanation: Azure helps provide network security for your environment by integrating a layered approach into the network architecture, which is an important part of securing the network from attacks and unauthorized access

Answers

VERSAtile Reads

431. Answer: C

Explanation: Microsoft Defender for Cloud is primarily used to identify internet-facing resources that are not secured properly. It helps in assessing resources that are exposed to the internet and ensures that inbound and outbound communication is restricted to only necessary ports and protocols.

432. Answer: D

Explanation: Azure Firewall is a managed, cloud-based network security service that provides a fully stateful firewall as a service with built-in high availability and unrestricted cloud scalability.

433. Answer: C

Explanation: Azure Application Gateway includes a Web Application Firewall (WAF) that offers centralized inbound protection of web applications from common exploits and vulnerabilities, specifically designed to protect HTTP traffic.

434. Answer: C

Explanation: Global VNet peering with Azure Firewall is supported but not recommended due to potential performance and latency issues that can arise across regions.

435. Answer: C

Explanation: Azure Firewall offers three types of rule collections: NAT rules (to forward traffic), Network rules (to allow traffic on specific IP ranges and ports), and Application rules (to allow applications or domain names to communicate across the network).

436. Answer: D

Explanation: Azure DDoS Protection is specifically designed to defend against denial of service attacks, where the goal is to overwhelm a network resource with excessive requests, making it slow or unresponsive.

437. Answer: B

Explanation: DDoS Protection Standard mitigates volumetric attacks, which aim to flood the network layer with a substantial amount of legitimate-looking traffic, by absorbing and scrubbing them using Azure's global network.

438. Answer: C

Explanation: When network traffic enters Azure Firewall, NAT rules are applied first. If the traffic matches a NAT rule, the firewall applies an implicit network rule for appropriate routing, and no further rule processing occurs.

439. Answer: C

Explanation: NSGs offer distributed network layer traffic filtering to limit traffic to resources within virtual networks. Azure Firewall is a centralized, stateful network firewall-as-a-service providing both network and application-level protection.

440. Answer: C

Explanation: Resource (application) layer attacks are aimed at web application packets to disrupt the transmission of data between hosts. These attacks include HTTP protocol violations, SQL injection, cross-site scripting, and other layer 7 attacks.

441. Answer: B

Explanation: Network Security Groups (NSGs) are critical for restricting communication between resources within an Azure virtual network to only what is necessary. They filter network traffic to and from Azure resources by source and destination IP address, port, and protocol.

442. Answer: C

Explanation: Azure service access can be limited to your virtual network by restricting access to service endpoints. This can help to remove public internet access to your services.

443. Answer: B

Explanation: Azure ExpressRoute is used to extend on-premises networks into the Microsoft cloud over a private connection facilitated by a connectivity provider, improving security by avoiding public internet.

444. Answer: C

Explanation: Azure Information Protection (AIP) can track and control how classified content is used, including analyzing data flows, detecting risky behaviors, tracking access, and preventing data leakage.

445. Answer: C

Explanation: Azure Information Protection uses Azure Rights Management (Azure RMS) to apply protection to documents and emails with encryption, identity, and authorization policies.

446. Answer: C

Explanation: Azure ExpressRoute facilitates private connections between your network and Azure, provided by a connectivity provider, avoiding the public internet.

447. Answer: C

Explanation: Azure Advanced Threat Protection aids security professionals by identifying, detecting, and investigating advanced threats, compromised identities, and malicious insider actions.

448. Answer: D

Explanation: The labels applied by Microsoft Azure Information Protection enable the control of access and usage of documents and emails, ensuring the protection of the data even outside the organization.

449. Answer: B

Explanation: Azure ExpressRoute improves the security of on-premises communication to Microsoft Cloud services by sending traffic over a private circuit instead of the public internet.

450. Answer: C

Explanation: Azure Advanced Threat Protection monitors users, entity behavior, and activities using learning-based analytics to help detect advanced attacks in hybrid environments.

451. Answer: C

Explanation: Policy assignment is the process of applying a policy definition within a certain scope, which can range from a full subscription down to a resource group. This ensures that the rules and standards defined in the policy are enforced within that scope.

452. Answer: C

Explanation: When a policy is assigned to a resource group, all child resources within that group inherit the policy assignment, meaning the rules apply to each resource within the group.

453. Answer: D

Explanation: Azure allows for the exclusion of sub-scopes when assigning policies. For instance, you can enforce a policy for an entire subscription and then exclude certain resource groups.

454. Answer: B

Explanation: Policies in Azure can be assigned through the Azure Portal, PowerShell, or Azure CLI, providing flexibility in how administrators manage policy assignments.

455. Answer: C

Explanation: The 'Deny' effect in Azure Policy will cause the resource creation or update to fail if the request violates the defined policy rules.

456. Answer: B

Explanation: The 'Audit' effect logs a warning event when a resource does not comply with the policy but does not prevent the resource from being created or updated.

457. Answer: C

Explanation: An initiative definition groups together a set of policy definitions to simplify management and to help track compliance against a broader objective.

458. Answer: C

Explanation: Initiatives are recommended to organize multiple policy definitions, especially when anticipating an increase in the number of policies.

459. Answer: C

Explanation: To find the Azure Policy section in the portal, you can use the search field or navigate to it through All Services.

460. Answer: D

Explanation: The 'DeployIfNotExists' effect allows Azure Policy to execute a template deployment to create or configure resources automatically when existing resources do not already meet certain conditions.

461. Answer: B

Explanation: Azure Blueprints maintain an active relationship with deployed resources, which is different from Azure Resource Manager Templates. This relationship is preserved even after deployment, aiding in improved tracking and auditing.

462. Answer: B

Explanation: Azure Blueprints enable development teams to rapidly build and deploy new environments with the knowledge that they're building within organizational compliance, thus increasing the speed of development and delivery.

463. Answer: C

Explanation: An Azure Blueprint can include a combination of resource groups, role assignments, policy assignments, and Azure Resource Manager templates as artifacts.

464. Answer: C

Explanation: Azure Resource Manager Templates are stored either locally or in source control, and once used for deployment, they have no active connection to the deployed resources. In contrast, Blueprints maintain a relationship with the resources after deployment.

465. Answer: C

Explanation: Role assignments in Azure Blueprints are used to add existing users or groups to a built-in role, ensuring that the right people always have the right access to the resources.

466. Answer: A

Explanation: Azure Blueprints can upgrade several subscriptions at once if they are governed by the same blueprint, which simplifies the management of multiple subscriptions.

467. Answer: C

Explanation: The Microsoft Trust Center is one of the sources provided by Microsoft to give full transparency on how the company manages the underlying resources that customers build upon.

468. Answer: A

Explanation: Virtual Networks are not listed as a supported artifact type in Azure Blueprint. The supported artifact types include resource groups, policy assignments, role assignments, and Azure Resource Manager templates.

469. Answer: B

Explanation: The Microsoft Privacy Statement explains what personal data Microsoft processes, how it's processed, and for what purposes, ensuring transparency in Microsoft's handling of personal data.

470. Answer: B

Explanation: The blueprint definition in Azure Blueprints specifies what resources should be deployed, and the blueprint assignment shows what resources were actually deployed, maintaining a clear relationship for improved tracking and auditing.

471. Answer: B

Explanation: Azure Monitor maximizes the availability and performance of applications by collecting, analyzing, and acting on telemetry from cloud and on-premises environments. It provides insights into how applications are performing and identifies issues affecting them and the resources they depend on.

.

472. Answer: C

Explanation: Azure Monitor collects metrics and logs from various tiers, including application monitoring data, guest OS monitoring data, Azure resource monitoring data, Azure subscription monitoring data, and Azure tenant monitoring data.

473. Answer: B

Explanation: Metrics are numerical values that describe some aspect of a system at a particular point in time. They are lightweight and capable of supporting near real-time scenarios.

474. Answer: C

Explanation: Azure Monitor for containers is designed to monitor the performance of container workloads deployed to managed Kubernetes clusters hosted on Azure Kubernetes Service (AKS).

475. Answer: C

Explanation: Application Insights is a service that monitors the availability, performance, and usage of web applications, whether hosted in the cloud or on-premises.

476. Answer: C

Explanation: Azure Monitor proactively notifies users of critical conditions using alerts, which can be based on metrics or logs. It also uses Auto-scale to adjust resources according to the load on the application.

477. Answer: B

Explanation: Azure Status provides a global view of the health state of Azure services and offers up-to-the-minute information on service availability.

478. Answer: B

Explanation: Azure Service Health provides personalized guidance and support when issues with Azure services affect users, including notifications, impact understanding, and updates on issue resolution.

479. Answer: C

Explanation: Resource Health helps diagnose and obtain support when an Azure service issue affects your resources, providing details about their current and past health states.

480. Answer: C

Explanation: Integrating monitoring services with Azure Service Health helps you stay informed of the health status of Azure services and understand if a broader Azure service issue is impacting your environment.

481. Answer: C

Explanation: Tags are used to organize resources within Azure for various purposes, such as billing and management. They allow you to group billing data, categorize costs, and retrieve related resources from different resource groups, which helps in monitoring and managing resources effectively.

482. Answer: B

Explanation: In a monitoring system, tags can be included with alerts to provide contextual information about which an issue may impact resources or departments. This helps in understanding the scope of a problem and aids in quicker resolution.

483. Answer: C

Explanation: Azure Policy can enforce rules for resource creation, such as only allowing specific types of resources to be created or limiting resources to specific Azure regions. It ensures compliance with organizational standards and regulatory requirements.

484. Answer: C

Explanation: Tags can be used in Azure Automation to automate the shutdown and startup of virtual machines based on specified times. For instance, tags like shutdown: 6 PM and startup: 7 AM can be used to save costs by shutting down and starting up VMs during off-hours.

485. Answer: C

Explanation: IT governance is about aligning IT initiatives with business goals to manage and prevent issues effectively. Azure Policy supports IT governance by allowing the creation and enforcement of policies that ensure resources comply with strategic objectives and standards.

486. Answer: B

Explanation: Azure Policy can restrict the deployment of resources to specific Azure regions, which is particularly useful for organizations with legal or regulatory restrictions on where data can reside, ensuring compliance with those requirements.

487. Answer: B

Explanation: Azure Policy can be used to restrict the deployment of larger, more expensive VM sizes in development environments, helping to minimize costs and prevent the use of unnecessary resources.

488. Answer: C

Explanation: Without standardized naming conventions, there can be inconsistencies in how resources are named across an Azure environment. Azure Policy can enforce naming conventions to ensure consistency and organization.

489. Answer: C

Explanation: When exporting billing data, including specific tags on resources allows for a more detailed and granular analysis of costs. Tags enable you to slice billing data in various ways to better understand and manage expenses.

490. Answer: C

Explanation: Tags are instrumental in the automation of operational tasks for virtual machines, such as shutting down and starting up VMs at specified times to optimize resource usage and reduce costs.

491. Answer: C

Explanation: To use the TCO calculator effectively, you must start by defining your workload. This involves entering details about your on-premises infrastructure, including servers, databases, storage, and networking.

492. Answer: C

Explanation: In the 'Servers' group, you should enter the details of your current on-premises server infrastructure to get an accurate cost comparison with Azure.

493. Answer: C

Explanation: For databases, you need to enter details in the 'Source' section about your on-premises database infrastructure and then select the corresponding Azure service in the 'Destination' section.

494. Answer: B

Explanation: You can adjust assumptions for storage costs, IT labor costs, hardware costs, software costs, and electricity costs to reflect the costs of your current on-premises infrastructure more accurately.

495. Answer: C

Explanation: The TCO calculator generates a report that enables you to compare the costs of your on-premises infrastructure with the costs of using Azure products and services to host your infrastructure in the cloud.

496. Answer: C

Explanation: Visual Studio subscribers can activate a monthly credit benefit, which allows them to experiment with, develop, and test new solutions on Azure without incurring monetary costs.

497. Answer: D

Explanation: When the Azure credit benefit is activated, the subscriber owns a separate Azure subscription under their account with a monthly credit balance that renews each month as long as they remain an active Visual Studio subscriber.

498. Answer: C

Explanation: Azure credits can be used to try out a wide range of services such as App Service, Windows 10 VMs, Azure SQL Server databases, Containers, Cognitive Services, Functions, Data Lake, and more.

499. Answer: C

Explanation: Adjusting the values of assumptions is essential to match the costs of your current on-premises infrastructure, which helps improve the accuracy of the TCO calculator.

500. Answer: C

Explanation: After creating cost estimates and analyzing where money is being spent, the next recommendation is to explore ways to reduce those infrastructure costs, which could include using Azure credits and optimizing resource usage

VERSAtile Reads

About Our Products

Other products from VERSAtile Reads are:

 Elevate Your Leadership: The 10 Must-Have Skills

 Elevate Your Leadership: 8 Effective Communication Skills

 Elevate Your Leadership: 10 Leadership Styles for Every Situation

 300+ PMP Practice Questions Aligned with PMBOK 7, Agile Methods, and Key Process Groups – 2024

 Exam-Cram Essentials Last-Minute Guide to Ace the PMP Exam - Your Express Guide featuring PMBOK® Guide

 Career Mastery Blueprint - Strategies for Success in Work and Business

 Memory Magic: Unraveling the Secret of Mind Mastery

 The Success Equation Psychological Foundations For Accomplishment

 Fairy Dust Chronicles – The Short and Sweet of Wonder

 B2B Breakthrough – Proven Strategies from Real-World Case Studies

CISSP Fast Track Master: CISSP Essentials for Exam Success

 CISA Fast Track Master: CISA Essentials for Exam Success

 CISM Fast Track Master: CISM Essentials for Exam Success

 CCSP Fast Track Master: CCSP Essentials for Exam Success

www.ingramcontent.com/pod-product-compliance
Lightning Source LLC
Chambersburg PA
CBHW060552060326
40690CB00017B/3685